THE WINNING DIALOGUE

The Winning Dialogue

Negotiation and communication for professionals

Thomas Benedict

You must be the change
you want to see in the world.
Mahatma Gandhi

Cover and inside design Simon van der Vegt

ISBN 1449963021

EAN 9781449963026

NUR 810, 765, 801

www.thewinningdialogue.com

Foreword

The basic principle behind this book is simple: 'know yourself and the other person.' We mostly know what we ourselves want, and where our own interests lie. But what about the other person, they have to look out for themselves, right? If that is how you think and act, then you are doing yourself a disservice.

If you want to do business with another person, focus on their situation and their interests. This vision provides a focal point for what professional conversations are all about. In the end, you are dependent on the other person to make a deal; so make sure you figure out what the other person needs. Then, where necessary, you can steer the conversation in a constructive direction. Both you and the other person benefit.

The theme of professional conversations is illuminated in depth in myriad ways in this book. 'Illuminated', because all possible aspects of a good professional conversation are brought to light and 'in depth', because various levels are addressed. Just by leafing through this book you will get a number of new ideas. The many practical tips included will definitely help. Take advantage!

Willem Mastenbroek

Preface

The Winning Dialogue has already helped thousands of people in dozens of different organizations to make a leap forward in their conversations and negotiations. Can it work for you as well? In order to help you determine the answer quickly, I present you with three questions.

1 *Do you work as a professional?*

I'm not talking about the title of your function, your position in the organization or your salary. David Maister wrote in *True Professionalism* (1997) about how professionals truly distinguish themselves: not so much through function, but through attitude. Whoever has a passion for his work and positions himself to serve in his surroundings is, as far as I'm concerned, a professional.

2 *Are conversations and negotiations important in your work?*

Conversations and negotiations are of essential importance for most functions. *The Winning Dialogue* is all about face to face conversations. Nevertheless, many of the concepts are useful if your communications take on another form.

3 *Are you open to becoming a better conversation partner and negotiator?*

The third question is the most important. Whoever is open to the growth and development of their competencies will get something out of every situation, every book and every training program that they are exposed to. For these people *The Winning Dialogue* is nothing less than a treasure trove of insights, overviews and connections most likely never made before. If you think that your conversations and negotiations are good enough as they are, maybe this book is not for you.

If you answered yes to these three questions, then it is definitely worth your while to read further.

For over fifteen years, I have trained a variety of professional groups, from doctors to accountants, from police officers to politicians, from managers to warehouse supervisors. After some time, I noticed that I was providing these diverse groups with the same kind of training and that there are a lot of similarities between leadership, sales, consulting, coaching, supervising, correcting, negotiating, and all the other aspects of business that people are occupied with on a daily basis. I discovered that while the *number of situations* is unlimited, the *type of communication* for these is not. Over the years, I have identified these types of communication and ranked them according to their priority in a conversation. That gave rise to a system of nine levels, ranging from dealing with aggression to making and concluding deals. I spent quite a lot of time testing if these nine levels were sufficient to help people of differing backgrounds to recognize and handle the most challenging situations. After years of honing the theory, the model is finished. It is the basis for training programs in the largest and best known organizations in the Netherlands and abroad. *The Winning Dialogue* works for whomever is prepared to invest the time in making it their own.

If you understand and master the winning dialogue system, you can add a number of especially useful tools to your toolbox:

1. You can easily describe, understand and influence complex and fast changing conversation and negotiation situations, no matter how unique they appear.
2. You can develop your own approach to the specific challenges of your branch, even if they are complicated or emotionally charged.
3. You can quickly shift if something suddenly changes during the course of a conversation or negotiation or if you encounter a block from the other person or within yourself.

4. You can easily recognize your own challenges and analyze and discuss these with others regardless of their field of expertise.
5. You can recognize and explain common problems in your conversations and use these as a starting point for personal growth.

In short, you get the overviews, the insights and the techniques – and you develop your own awareness – to bring your conversations to a higher level.

How to use the book

This book contains a lot of information. You can of course read it from cover to cover, but I would advise you to read Part I about the theory and the underlying principles of the model first. Thereafter, you can determine where your challenges may lie and from there further study the information relevant to you in Part II. According to your needs and the situations that you encounter in your daily routine, you can use this book as a reference and look up new subjects as they become relevant.

In conclusion

This book is about negotiation and is aimed at professionals, regardless of their field of expertise. Although the system can also be used in your personal life, it is primarily focused on business situations. The complex conversations you conduct in your private life, for example, settling conflicts or negotiating a sale or purchase, definitely fall within the framework of this book, but are not handled explicitly.

For the sake of simplicity this book assumes a dialogue between two people. Most structures, skills and tips are also applicable where more people are involved.

Part I

Introduction to the model

1

The Winning Dialogue: basic principles

In his impressive book *The Seven Habits of Highly Effective People*, Stephen Covey (2000) distinguishes between blindly employing tricks of the trade on the one hand and following principles based on insights which fit in with your own values on the other. He argues that people should only apply these principles, which are based on values such as fairness, integrity, human dignity, service, trust and mutual dependence, once they understand and can really identify with each one. According to Covey, learning and unthinkingly executing superficial tricks, without knowing and supporting the underlying principles behind them leads to a less effective performance. The same idea of personal commitment is also a basic principle of the winning dialogue system.

I am convinced that the effectiveness of a model is determined to a large extent by the degree to which the user can relate to the ideas behind it. My advice then is that you evaluate every technique or skill to decide whether it fits in with your ideas about what is possible, acceptable, what works and what does not. In this way, you ensure that you do not employ tricks that are not part of who you are, but you do use techniques which help you to give better form to what you do believe in. The winning dialogue system was developed based on five basic principles, which will be further outlined below. Before you get immersed in how this model operates, it is important to determine for yourself if you can identify with these principles. Only then will you be able to apply the system effectively.

The basic principles of a winning dialogue are:

1. Live in the moment
2. Act proactively

3. Focus on the other person
4. Earn the right to the next step
5. Work non-manipulatively

Live in the moment

People lose a lot of concentration and efficiency by dwelling on the past or worrying about the future (Tolle, 2005). This means that they miss the most important moment of influence, the now, and therefore the chance to really shape their situation. The more you are able to concentrate your capacities, the more effective and enjoyable your efforts will be. The past has brought you to where you are now, but it is unchangeable. The future is undetermined, but can only be influenced to a certain extent. The answer to the question of how much you can influence your future depends on the degree to which and the way in which you function in the now.

If you limit conversations to the here and now, you are not involved in settling old scores or worrying about what could happen in the future. Rather, you are focused on what is happening right now. That is not to say that reflecting on the past or making future plans is never relevant. Reflection and planning both have their place, as long as you are choosing to engage in these activities in the here and now and can stop doing so after an appropriate length of time. Concluding reflection or planning well contributes to the effectiveness of your performance. However, if thinking about the past or the future turns into a constant gnawing undertone, then it becomes a hindrance.

Act proactively

Situations in which you are communicating with others are constantly changing, not least because you are influencing the situation yourself. What you say and how you say it has influence on the other person

– just as the other person influences you with their communication. But whatever they say or do, you are always in a position to choose how you will react to it. This choice and the resulting freedom and responsibility form the basis for proactive behaviour. Prior to each action or interaction, there is always a moment of choice that is not always experienced as such, or exploited optimally. Using your awareness and moments of choice, especially in difficult or challenging situations, determines your attitude and the meaning you assign to the situation and the role which you play in it. Many times people justify negative, manipulative, emotional or aggressive behaviour by citing the circumstances or another person's behaviour. Another's behaviour leads to an automatic reaction, as if not they themselves, but outside factors have caused their behaviour. But in reality, no one is an automated responder: we all give direction to our own behaviour and are therefore responsible for it. We are free to determine our behaviour, to direct our energies and to experience the consequences – both positive and negative (Covey, 2000). Most people understand this insight, in theory. But in daily life, recognizing moments of choice, consciously choosing and accepting responsibility for choices made demands a large dose of discipline and dedication. This book and the strategies described within it assume that you are aware of the fact that you make your own choices and therefore determine your own behaviour.

Focus on the other person

Who determines if you will be successful in achieving your goals? An order that goes through, a staff member who gets motivated, a client who really lets you into their world – these are all processes taking place with your conversation partner, not yourself. The other person, in fact, holds the key to your success. This surprising insight, called 'allocentrism'* by Nalebuff and Brandenburger (1996) in their

* Literally: putting the other person in the centre, from the Greek 'allos': another and 'centrism': positioning in the centre.

book *Co-opetition*, is of essential importance for conducting effective negotiations. It implies namely that you have to focus quite a lot of attention on the interests, the situation, the feelings, and the personality of your conversation partner. Because the better you are able to put yourself in the other person's shoes, the closer you will come to the source of your success. And the better you are able to conduct your conversations based on this basic principle, the more effective and successful you will be.

Earn the right to the next step

Working step by step is more or less a continuation of what has taken place previously. This also comes down to the idea that the things you say and do during a conversation should be relevant to your conversation partner's experiences. This is not only true of the content (as outlined in the previous principle), but also for the timing and the sequence in which you address each issue. When your actions do not appear consistent or if you do not take enough time to let things sink in, you run the risk of your conversation partner losing interest, and, even in the most favourable case, will cost you extra energy to reach your goal. By working step by step, you create the opportunity for yourself to focus on the other person and remain flexible.

You can view a successful conversation as a process of continuous steps that bring you ever closer to your goal. With each correct step, you create as it were an opening with the other person to take the next step. In that way, you are building little by little a firm foundation for the results which you are trying to achieve. For example, during a sales conversation, a good opening creates the opportunity to ask questions. By listening to the answers, you can further recommend your products with the correct approach. If you present an appropriate proposal, the client will be prepared to negotiate. With this trajectory, you create step by step the opportunity to write out the order.

Another example: one of your staff is angry and appears de-motivated. By listening to their story and taking their emotions seriously, not only do you find out what is going on exactly, but you also win their trust. And from this position, you have the opportunity to influence the situation, for example by thinking together and coming up with a solution. Eventually, you can come to mutual agreements which will remove the dissatisfaction of your staff member.

With a clear, step by step structure and conscious moments of control, you can maintain contact with your conversation partner and give yourself the chance to make optimum use of your opportunities in the conversation.

Work non-manipulatively

During the training sessions that I facilitate, I often notice that people are interested in learning techniques with which they can trump their conversation partners or pressure them. But these types of techniques do not honour the two-sided nature of the communication process and, as far as I am concerned, are even damaging to the mutual trust which is necessary to a joint achievement.

Communication is a powerful tool which can help you influence others to a large degree. By comprehending the basic principles of effective communication – with the aid of this book for example – you have formidable means at your disposal. That brings with it its own danger, namely the conscious, destructive use of your communicative power to manipulate others. Manipulation in this case means the use of tricks which aim to limit the freedom of choice of others.

Sometimes, the difference between effective communication and manipulation can be difficult to determine. If you withhold or distort information, introduce artificial time pressure to a conversation, sow confusion or exploit the weaknesses, fears or worries of your conversation partner in order to limit her freedom of choice, then you are being manipulative. Then it will be no surprise that the other person has the feeling that the conversation was less than fair. Again, this does not mean that you should not make use of your influence or get into vigorous negotiation with someone.

If you are prone to taking people off guard or using other means of pressure, it might be helpful to examine where this urge comes from. You will probably discover that, as for many others, it is rooted in a lack of confidence in the situation or in the willingness of your conversation partner. This lack of confidence is not always explicit, recognizable or realistic: experiences and emotions from the past influence your behaviour and can, without your being aware of it, influence your thoughts and actions.

Many people use manipulative techniques, especially in situations where the stakes are high and where they have a feeling of powerlessness or lack of influence. If you recognize yourself in this, then I would like to ask you: do you like what you're doing? But also: is it really working for you? If you manipulate your conversation partners, they will – based on your actual behaviour and therefore in a certain sense justifiably – judge you as 'untrustworthy' or 'threatening'. They will also react accordingly, for example, by digging in their heels. And thus a vicious cycle arises: your lack of confidence is 'confirmed' and you encounter a self-fulfilling prophecy.

Nearly all conversations can be brought to a positive conclusion in an honest, respectful manner, even the traditionally complex or 'hard' situations such as (commercial) negotiations. By exploring and weighing each other's interests and making concessions, negotiation partners create an opening for agreement. Personally, I prefer giving concessions to people that I like, or at least people who act with integrity, rather than to people who play tricks on me or place me under undue pressure.

2

The winning dialogue system

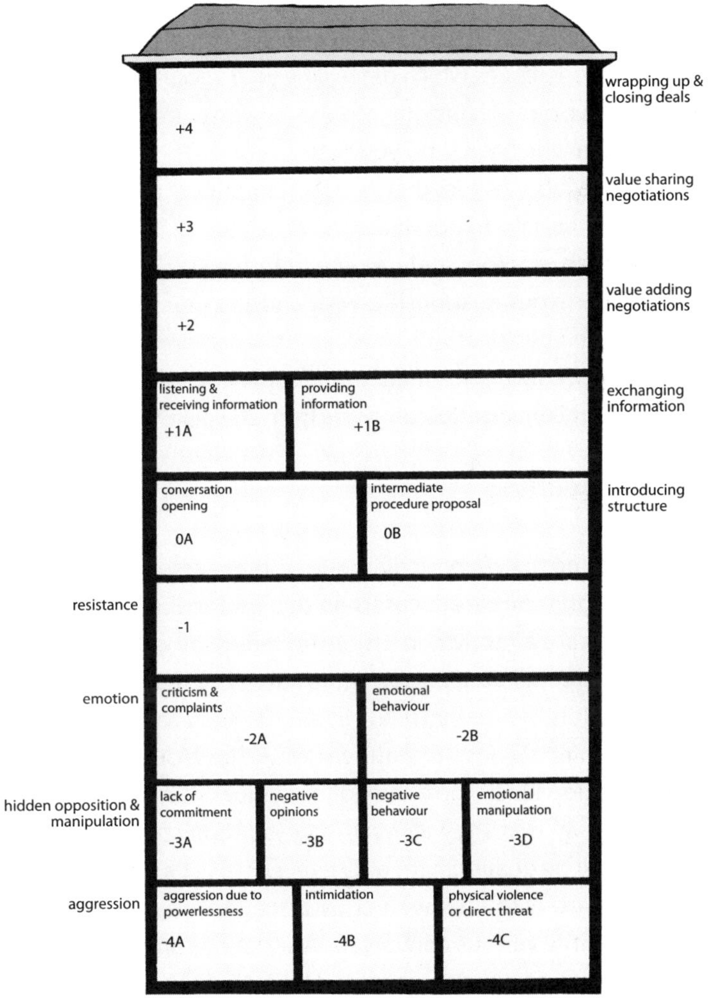

Although the number of situations in which you communicate with others is quite large, the different types of communication are limited. Your role – whether you are a salesperson, a client, a manager or staff member – and your relationship with your conversation partner – be it a professional, friendly, casual or pleasant relationship – define the framework of the conversation. Furthermore, situations involving communication exhibit certain important similarities. The winning dialogue system provides you with tips for performing effectively in all possible types of situations. Issues which determine your success include:

- Do you have enough insight into the conversation or negotiation situation in which you find yourself?
- Are you capable of recognizing your emotions and using them without letting them dominate the situation?
- Do you react appropriately, in line with the situation, your role, your values, your relationship with and the perspective of your conversation partner?
- Does your performance match up with your goals and interests, even if your conversation diverges from the plan?

Floors of a Building

While developing the winning dialogue system, I assumed conversations and negotiations are focused on the joint realisation of goals. I wanted to create a model: an insightful reflection of reality which can be applied to all conceivable situations. The result is a system that, because it is divided into levels, can be seen as an apartment building with nine stories – five above ground and four below. These nine conversation levels form the building blocks of a conversation. That is not to say that they all occur in every conversation; almost always, you will be dealing with only a few levels at a time. Together they provide you with a conveniently arranged system which you can use to identify various conversation situations and teach you to determine what has priority when and why.

The division between above ground and below ground has been consciously chosen. The underground levels are *condition forming*, which is to say that there you lay the groundwork to be effective in the above ground levels. You do that by noticing negative signals in a conversation and processing these. Above ground levels are target oriented: they help you to achieve what you are working towards.

The four underground stories – the condition forming levels – relate to negative situations or barriers which can frustrate your conversation in any number of ways. This means conversation situations that are in general difficult to handle, often containing an emotional undertone, which can have an obstructive or even disabling effect on your desired results. Clearing these types of barriers is an essential condition for developing a constructive conversation.

On the ground floor, (level 0 of the system) you make agreements about the structure and the content of the conversation. This level is not only relevant to the beginning of a conversation, but also the transition from a condition forming level to a constructive level. After you have smoothed over a relatively rough situation to the satisfaction of your conversation partner, it is helpful to present him with your ideas about the subsequent structure of the conversation.

The four stories above ground comprise the techniques for constructive communication: from creating structure on the ground floor, to wrapping up and closing deals on the fourth floor. These are the constructive conversation levels.

The various conversation levels are explained in greater detail in Part II. You will find the complete diagram in appendix 1.

Rules of use: necessity, priority and freedom

There are three rules for effective use of the winning dialogue system:

- Necessity
- Priority
- Freedom

Necessity

With the winning dialogue system, you only use the conversation levels that you need. Your estimation of the situation(s) and your choice not to focus too much attention and priority on unnecessary aspects is reflected in the flexibility which is characteristic of the system. You are therefore never obligated to do anything just because it is prescribed in the system. The motto is: use what you need – and leave the rest.

Priority

The various conversation levels in the winning dialogue system are arranged so that situations with the highest priority are addressed in the lower levels of the model. You always work from bottom to top. This sequence is based on the fact that stressful, challenging situations must be resolved before you can continue on to less tense situations. For example, if there is any intimidation (level -4, aggression) and anger (level -2, emotions), then according to the rule of priority, you would first focus on the intimidation. As soon as you have dealt with that, you can turn to addressing your conversation partner's anger.

This rule of priority is also applicable to the above ground levels. There, it is no longer about removing or reducing tension, but earning the right to take the next step. In an advisory conversation for example, the opening (level 0, creating structure) leads to the right to ask questions (level +1) and finally to providing advice (level +1). Value adding negotiations/problem solving (level +2) come before value sharing negotiations (level +3), because it is better to explore solutions which provide mutual advantages before moving on to sharing the rewards.

If during a conversation you notice that you still need to resolve an issue at a lower level, the order in which you address things is important. An example: you are in a tough negotiation with your client and are looking for ways to solve problems with cooperation (level +2, value adding negotiations/problem solving). If you feel that you need to solidify the deals made (level +4, wrapping up and making deals), then you can easily postpone that until you have finished working on level +2; level +2 is after all lower in the model than level +4. It is another thing altogether if your partner's emotions flare up while coming together on level +2. The best way to continue the conversation is by immediately shifting back to level -2 (emotion), because level -2 is lower than level +2. So if over the course of the conversation you come to an issue that is lower than level you are on: immediately shift down to the lower level before moving back to the level where you were. This flexibility ensures that you can optimally connect to the situation and your conversation partner at any moment, which will ultimately make your conversation more successful.

It is up to you to apply the rule of priority. You can of course choose to ignore a stressful situation from a lower level, but be aware that by doing so you risk the rest of the conversation going sour and not reaching your target. If, over the course of a conversation, you encounter behaviour from a lower level, then the best response is to stop and switch to that lower level. Afterwards, you can move back to the original, higher level you were at in order to work towards realizing your goals. In this way, you create the conditions to get what you want out of a conversation without damaging your integrity or your relationship with the other person.

Freedom

The guiding principle of the winning dialogue system is that you have the freedom to determine what you do and when. You make choices based on your observations: the choice not to discuss certain subjects, the choice not to focus attention somewhere and the choice of what level of conversation you want to work on. You yourself make the decision. Your decisions do involve responsibilities: you are responsible for what you do and for the consequences of your actions. Undoubtedly there will come a time when you cause a negative reaction in your conversation partner. It is up to you to figure out your role in this result and to take appropriate action, and, if possible, to learn from the mistake.

3

Preparation

After a general introduction about the system and the way in which you can use it, it is time to get to grips with its application. To do so, you work with three phases:

1. Preparation
2. Conducting the conversation
3. Evaluation & reflection

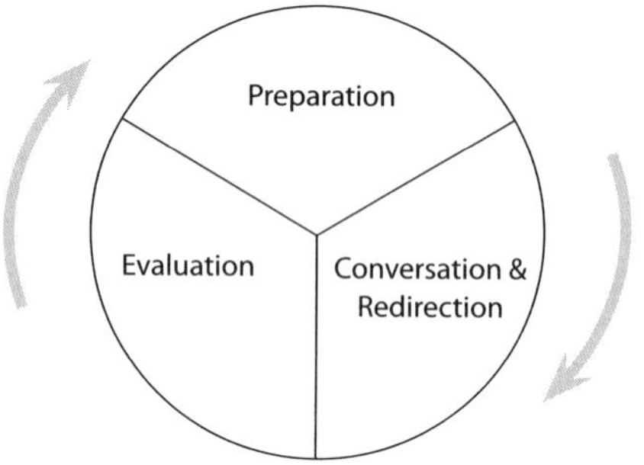

Figure 1 The three phases of working with the winning dialogue system

This chapter deals with the first phase, preparation. The phases of conversation and evaluation & reflection will be addressed in the following chapters.

Even before you begin a conversation, you can already do a number of things to positively influence the course of the conversation. A valuable part of your preparation is to think about the structure of the conversation beforehand. The winning dialogue system lends itself well to this practice – you could say it invites you to do so. Up to now, you may have worked with established conversation structures you don't really have to think about, but with the winning dialogue system, you are going to determine the structure yourself. You are not carrying out something someone else has thought of, but developing a structure that fits with your wishes and expectations of the situation. Thinking about and determining the structure beforehand can have the positive effect of making you aware of alternative routes, should your original choice (no longer) be the best. That may be because your estimation of the situation was not correct or because the conversation took an unexpected turn. This flexibility is an important advantage of using the winning dialogue system rather than more general and rigid conversation models. There is one more advantage: if you are the architect of your own conversations, you give your conversations a personal signature. In that way, the reactions you draw from others will fit with who you are and the experience you gain is more relevant to you.

The preparation for a conversation with the winning dialogue system as a guideline consists of three steps. First, assess the situation, second, set goals and last, determine your approach.

Assess the situation: what is going on?

The first step in the preparation for a conversation is assessing the situation. By answering the following questions you can sketch a detailed outline of the starting position of the conversation:

- Which issues play a role between you and your conversation partner?
- Which interests do you represent in your contact with the other person?
- Whose interests are they?
- Which role do you play with regard to your conversation partner?
- How has your relationship with the other person been up to now?
- Which emotions play a role for you and your conversation partner?
- What is the balance of power between you both?
- How do you see your dependence on the other?
- To what degree do you view the other as helpful/responsive?
- How much confidence do you have in the other person?

- To what degree do you experience your relationship with the other as stressful or contentious?

You can increase your chance of success not only by answering these questions for yourself and thereby clarifying your own perspective, but by guessing at your partner's answers to the same questions and thus gaining an idea of his perspective.

Set goals: what do I want to achieve?

The more specifically you determine your goals, the better you can work towards achieving them – and the better able you will be to evaluate your success afterwards. Setting goals beforehand helps you to learn from a conversation afterwards.

Goals can be divided into three categories: concrete, relationship oriented and process related goals. 'Concrete goals' are the most common and have to do with the professional results of your conversation. For example, you want to land an order, gain acceptance of advice or make a favourable deal. The second area in which you can set goals is in the quality of your relationship with another person. For similar 'relationship oriented goals' you want answers to questions like: How does the other person see me? Do people view me as a slick salesman or an advisor? Am I credible enough to negotiate on behalf of my organization? Do people view me as a troublemaker or are my concerns taken seriously? Does the other person see me as a partner or an enemy? The third type of goal, the 'process related goal', is focused on the progression of the interaction between you and your conversation partner. Issues at play can include: Is the other person prepared to lay their real concerns and interests on the table in this conversation? Can I identify my client's personal concerns? Is the client ready to hear my advice? Or: is the other person ready for a follow up conversation?

Most people are inclined to give concrete goals priority and treat the other types of goals as a means to an end. But experience teaches us that aspects such as your reputation as a professional and the degree to which people build trust in you over time are much more important in the long term than short term, concrete goals. Always try to keep in mind what consequences it can have for a long term relationship if you only strive for specific (especially concrete) goals. That will help you make decisions about what priority you assign to your conversation goals.

But it is not sufficient to only look at yourself and work on your goals. For a successful negotiation you have to (in any case) determine what the other person would like to achieve in their contact with you. By examining yourself, the relationship and the goals from the other person's perspective you can make a good estimation of the manner in which the other person sees their contact with you. This enables you to look at how you can achieve your goals, but also what obstacles you might expect to come across in the course of the conversation.

Preparing to address certain topics, challenges and issues with the winning dialogue system: how do I approach this?

After you have evaluated the situation and established your goals, you can determine which subjects you need to discuss. If you're smart, at this stage you will consider difficult points which might come up. By examining these issues beforehand, using the winning dialogue system you can decide which subjects you want to address in which order (taking priority into account). Further on in this book you will find tips for concrete and process related preparation applicable to each conversation level (read: every conversation situation).

Table 1 shows which interaction levels match your topics, issues or challenges and therefore which levels are relevant to the conversation in question.

Your assessment/expectation of the conversation	**Conversation Level**
• Your goals and those of your conversation partner are widely divergent • Your interests and those of the other person are so far apart that without tough negotiations you will never reach a comprise • Your conversation partner and you both represent parties who expect the best possible result • You have to reach a mutual solution with someone you know to be an ambitious negotiator • You have to reach an agreement with your conversation partner, but you have no further relationship with him • You need to resolve certain issues and are very tense around your conversation partner	**+3** **value sharing negotiations**
• You expect to encounter complex issues • You know that resolving negotiation issues with your conversation partner is possible and you have a family or professional relationship with one another • It is important for you to reach a solution, but you are not clear on where the other party's interests lie	**+2** **value adding negotiations/ problem solving**
• You would like to convince your conversation partner of something • You would like to sell something to the other person • You would like your conversation partner to take your advice	**+1B2** **persuasion and advice**
• You need to teach your conversation partner something • You would like to transfer information • You are giving instructions	**+1B1** **providing information**
• You want to gather information from the other person • You would like to know the other person's views on a certain issue • You want the other person to have the feeling that you are listening (you want to build confidence)	**+1A** **listening, receiving information**

Your assessment/expectation of the conversation	Conversation Level
• The sequence of and subjects to be discussed in a conversation are of great importance for (one of) the parties involved • You expect the conversation to be complicated • You expect one of the parties – for whatever reason – will be sensitive to the conversation and the subjects addressed therein • It will more or less be a formal conversation • You know that important interests are at stake	**0A conversation opening**
• You expect resistance or objection to what you want to suggest • You expect resistance or objection to the procedure or another aspect of the conversation • You know the other person is resistant to you or the organization you represent	**-1 resistance**
• You are the bearer of bad news • You expect – for whatever reason – criticism or complaints • You suspect that your conversation partner will become emotional	**-2 emotion**
• You expect that your conversation partner is not enthusiastic about the conversation • You know that your interest in the conversation is greater than that of your partner • You expect your conversation partner does not want contact with you or has difficulty with one of the subjects you wish to discuss	**-3A lack of commitment**
• You presume that the other person blames you for things • You have done or neglected to do things in the past that the other person holds against you	**-3B negative opinions about you**

Your assessment/expectation of the conversation	Conversation Level
You cannot prepare for negative behaviour	**-3C negative behaviour**
• There is a large discrepancy in the balance of power • You know that the other person needs something from you or is in another way dependent on you • You suspect that the other person thinks you are difficult to influence • You feel dependent on the approval or acceptance of your conversation partner	**-3D emotional manipulation**
• You have to work within guidelines or limitations • You represent an organization that has power over your conversation partner • You have control of resources, expertise, services or goods which your partner desperately needs • You have reason to assume that your conversation partner thinks of you as inaccessible, difficult to influence or arrogant • You feel that your conversation partner exceeded your limits in the past • You are nervous or fearful of undertaking the conversation	**-4A or B aggression due to powerlessness or intimidation**

Table 1 Expectations and conversation levels

4

Conducting the Conversation

After thorough preparation, you are ready for the conversation. Chances are that you will immediately benefit from your hard work: portions of your conversation go much smoother than you had expected and before you know it, you have concluded business to everyone's satisfaction. Other subjects may take a little more time and effort than expected. You may possibly have to adjust your goals or realize that your expectations of the conversation do not square with the reality.

No matter how well you prepare for a conversation, unforeseen situations can always come up. It can be difficult to deal with these appropriately, especially if they are caused by your conversation partner. If you are still relatively inexperienced in conducting conversations according to the winning dialogue system, just learning to recognize unexpected, negative shifts in a conversation can be advantageous. To do so, it is not only necessary to monitor the behaviour of the other person, but also to stay in touch with your own feelings. Only when you know exactly what is going on are you capable of reacting appropriately. The winning dialogue system leaves room for the necessary flexibility: at any moment, you can deviate from your original plan and redirect the conversation and then subsequently pick up where you left off.

One example of a situation that requires redirection is the unexpected bad reception of a proposition during a negotiation. Rather than simply dismissing the proposal and continuing towards an acceptable resolution, your conversation partner reacts angrily and feels insulted and this prevents you from negotiating realistically. Maybe his reaction shocks you or you become angry because you feel it is unfounded. In this case, it is wise not to express your feelings right away, but to learn to recognize and use them as a sign that the conversation is not going as planned and therefore the structure needs to be revaluated. If at this juncture you persist with your original plan and continue with negotiations, chances are that your emotions or those of your conversation partner will have an obstructive effect on the progress of the negotiation. The other person might harbour bitterness and refuse to look for a solution which is satisfactory to you. There is also the possibility that your emotions get the better of you and the situation gets out of hand. By immediately responding to the insulted reaction of the other person you create an environment where the chance of a successful conclusion of the negotiation is much greater. You shift to another level of the model: you stop negotiation (level +2 or +3) and begin dealing with emotions (level -2). Only when the other person has calmed down and vented their feelings can you continue where you left off in a constructive manner.

The opportunity to redirect a conversation at any time and give temporary priority to dealing with a problem is characteristic of the winning dialogue system's flexibility. Redirection is in fact nothing other than consciously applying the system during a conversation. In order to do this well, you have to make the system your own, develop a bird's-eye view, and learn to use your own feelings as a guide.

You will find a schematic overview of the winning dialogue system in appendix 1.

In order to achieve the best results with the winning dialogue system, I advise you not only to learn more about the actual model, but also to develop insights into the ways in which it can be used and – at least as important – in what happens with yourself and your conversation partner during a conversation. That is not to say that you can only work with the system effectively once you can do that. From the moment you first apply the basic principles of the system, you and your conversation partner will undoubtedly benefit. A conversation held according to the winning dialogue system, acknowledges everything that happens in the dialogue, but allows you to always return to constructive progress.

5

Evaluation & reflection

'Learning by doing' definitely applies to working with the winning dialogue system. It starts with consistently evaluating conversations you have had: don't just focus on whether or not you have achieved your goal, but try to analyze *how* you did so. Would you have come as far – or maybe even farther – more easily or with less stress by using another approach? Only thorough and honest evaluation will help you to learn from your conversations. In this chapter you will read how you can structure your learning process based on this system.

By working with the winning dialogue system, not only do you learn about the model, you also learn more about yourself. You can gain different levels of learning from what took place in a conversation, whether they are ideas directly applicable to the conversation which will help you move forward or profound insights about yourself. Gradually, you will gain insight in the following levels of learning:

- The playing field
- The other person
- The interaction
- Yourself

Just like the metaphor of the winning dialogue system – the building where you (in principle) work from bottom to top – you can view the degree to which you attain insights into the various levels as a stairway you are climbing. The lowest level is relatively easy to comprehend and, despite its importance, has less impact on the higher levels. As you increase your knowledge of the higher levels, you experience more opportunities for influence. Understanding the higher levels enriches your understanding of the lower levels. In this way, your knowledge of interaction (level 3) enhances your insights about the other person (level 2) and the situation (level 1). It will not surprise you that the higher levels cannot be mastered in an afternoon. The levels concerning interaction and insight into yourself are difficult to grasp.

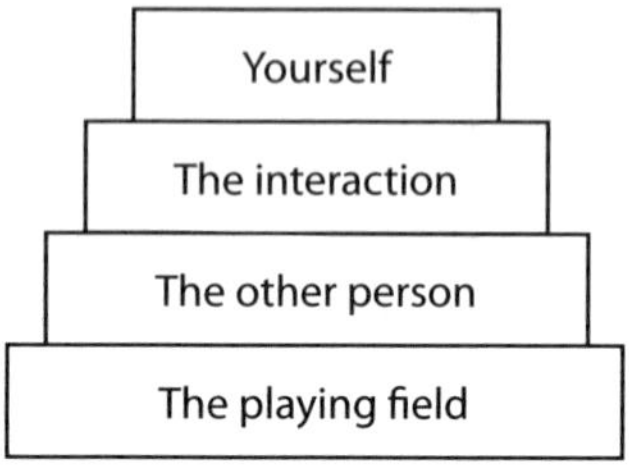

Figure 1 Levels of learning

The playing field

By reflecting on the factors that influence the content and course of a conversation, you become aware of the playing field. Think for example about the background and interests of your conversation partner, your history together, and the topics which will come up during the conversation. The better able you are to survey the playing field, the easier it will be to determine an effective structure for the conversation. And, equally important, the better prepared you will be for unexpected events.

The other person

The capacity to be empathetic enables you to place yourself in the other person's shoes. This is a useful skill, especially in a difficult conversation or negotiation, because it helps you to evaluate what your conversation partner needs from you in order to proceed. Thanks to your ability to imagine the other person's point of view, you can be more confident in conversations with others.

The more you open yourself up to your conversation partners, the more signals you will receive from them – signals which can help you approach them in the correct manner. That is easier to do when you value the other person and are sincerely interested in them. The more tense your relationship is, the more challenging it will be to open up to the other person and paradoxically enough, the more important it becomes to pick up their signals. In stressful situations, the subtle information you receive can help you find an opening.

The interaction

In each conversation you are dealing with two or more people, each with their own set of experiences and frame of reference. Differences make our communications complex, even when we are not aware of it.

Additionally, a conversation is a continual process of reciprocal influence on various levels. Your conversation partner responds to you and you in turn respond back. Unravelling this fleeting interaction provides a number of insights into the course of a conversation and especially where it can go wrong. These types of insights are important because they help you understand what effect subtle signals have on you – and on the other person. In this way you can continually fine tune your behaviour and create the desired effects in your conversations. Your conversation partner's reactions provide you with constant feedback about your communication. This shows you which reactions are triggered by the signals you send out and what works in certain situations and what does not.

Yourself

In your communications with your environment, you demonstrate who you are. You have the opportunity to use your talents, realize your resolutions and apply lessons learned. Your interactions with others can also confront you with your weaknesses. This is unavoidable and at the same time valuable. This is the point at which you can learn the most: your mistakes provide you with the greatest opportunity for growth.

Working with your feelings

While I was developing the winning dialogue system, I only focused on your feelings, your resistance, your aggression and your tendency to manipulate to a limited degree. This is no accident. Naturally you are only human and these characteristics are not foreign to you. Still, I assume that you are professional enough to strive towards keeping your emotions from playing an overriding or negative role in your conversations.

You have an emotional life which is not always immediately visible, but which does strongly influence your behaviour. This means that your emotions are essential to your performance. They can help you get better at applying the winning dialogue system and noticing even the most subtle signals which come up over the course of a conversation. While cutting off your feelings altogether seems an attractive idea, it is never the best solution. This is because your feelings usually tell you infallibly if you are being manipulated or if the conversation has derailed. If you lose contact with your feelings, then you are not capable of really understanding what is going on under the surface of the conversation.

On the other hand, your feelings can have a negative impact: they can mislead you or cause you to react (too) emotionally. For example, if your conversation partner becomes emotional and you do too, this will have an escalating effect on the conversation. There is an art to using your feelings positively – as an indicator, to register your position in the conversation in relation to the other person and to remain in control of your emotions.

Learning at this level means analyzing which situations bring about which emotions for you. If you want to do this well, then it is important to develop the discipline to distinguish between feelings which (in nature and intensity) have to do with the situation at hand and feelings which are in fact memories which you unconsciously associate with the situation but which rationally seen – especially from the perspective of your conversation partner – have nothing specific to do with the situation here and now. If you react according to the 'attached emotion', you can almost be sure that the other person will not follow you and will get the feeling that you are overreacting. After all, you are not reacting to what is actually happening, but to something that is entirely unrelated to the here and now.

By being aware of what types of situations give rise to you having 'associated emotions,' you are taking a big step in the right direction. Then you can be extra careful or take responsibility for your emotions, rather than allowing the emotions to take control of you. You could go a step farther and scrutinize your unconscious emotions, those which are lying in wait for a situation with which you can associate them. If you can gain insight into them, you can make better use of your emotions in your conversations and gain more confidence in acting on your feelings.

Images

If you focus on getting to know your emotional life, you will notice that you have difficulty again and again with certain challenges and specific situations. The winning dialogue system offers you a useful framework which helps you to recognize this more quickly and with greater certainty. If you are open to the process, you can use the confrontations with your environment in the form of conversations to learn more about yourself; about your motives, your strengths and your weaknesses. But especially about your images: the specific manner in which you view the world.

Images are a person's accepted 'truths' which determine how he interprets situations and events. Early in life everybody develops images about how the world works and how you as a person can deal with it. These images determine the manner in which we experience things and how we handle them. Most images are true and correct and help us progress. But some images are based on misunderstanding and confusion. At the time they were developed, they may have played an important part in dealing with a difficult situation. But images can become lodged in your subconscious and from this unseen position determine your observations and behaviour. After a certain amount of time, they are no longer necessary and even become damaging, but still exert a powerful – counterproductive – influence.

Recurring problems or situations which you constantly wrestle with, point to the presence of 'outdated images.' They cause you to waste a lot of energy: while you may be striving vigorously for a certain result, an opposing image can cause you to run in circles again and again. 'Outdated images' make your behaviour rigid and incomprehensible to others. They can pull the rug out from under you and make it difficult to have pleasant and constructive conversations with people.

Typical examples of images which can have an effect on a conversation through underlying feelings:

- 'Do not provide too much information about yourself.'
- 'Trust no one.'
- 'Get what you can, while you can.'
- 'You must never ask questions.'
- 'Emotions are worthless, exhibiting them is weak.'
- 'Authority figures only want to hurt you.'
- 'You have to force people to give you what you want.'

In practice, you may wonder if it is coincidental that you often end up in the same situation. Many people believe that unexpected meetings and other occurrences are not coincidental, but have a purpose. According to them, people create their own experiences based on what is going on inside them. They see the world around every person as a projection of their inner state. With positive, integrated elements, they create positive experiences and with conflicting, negative elements, they attract conflicting and negative situations. Whether or not you choose to believe this – it is beyond dispute that we have a certain influence on what we experience. It is up to you to decide to what degree you wish to apply this idea to your life and your communications with others.

A good way to find out what images you have is by focussing on your themes, and carefully examining them: what stumbling blocks keep tripping you up, what feedback do you always get from other people, what conversation levels remain difficult for you? The information in the paragraph beginning with 'Difficulty with...' which closes each chapter in Part II, can help you take the first step in recognizing and understanding your personal images and themes. An exciting investigation of yourself, with valuable insights as a result!

Part II The winning dialogue explained in detail

In this part of the book, each conversation level will be discussed separately from the inception, preparation and introduction to the subsequent steps, including any problems you may encounter and possible solutions for these. Each level is illustrated with a number of examples of conversation situations.

It was a conscious choice to begin with the underground levels in dealing with the various conversation levels. An effective handling of these levels – should they be relevant – is conditional to successfully completing the constructive levels: the levels where you can reach concrete professional results.

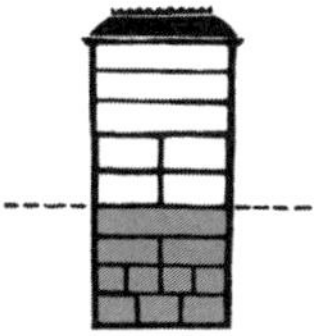

6

Condition forming conversation levels (-4 through -1)

The four condition forming conversation levels of the winning dialogue system have one thing in common: at first glance, professionally speaking, you do not seem to be achieving a huge amount. But what you are able to achieve shapes the rest of the conversation. Situations on condition forming levels present a very real barrier to a constructive professional conversation. For example, when you come across emotion or resistance in a conversation, you will not be able to move on until you have addressed the issue in a manner which is satisfying to the other person. A condition forming situation which receives little or no attention can result in you not reaching your goals. If such a situation forms a barrier to you achieving your goals, then it should have a high priority for you.

Again, the condition forming conversation levels are not underground for nothing: they are not always observed or consciously recognized in a conversation, let alone dealt with in an effective way. That is why in preparing for a conversation it is a good idea to assess the odds of having to deal with a condition forming level so that you can take it into account.

Table 1 indicates per conversation level, which specific level you need to work on. The levels of learning discussed in the previous chapter (yourself, the other person, the interaction and the playing field) are the points of departure for this. The interaction level of learning does not appear in the diagram, because there is as yet no interaction. That does not mean however that the interaction is not a determining factor in the development of the conversation, for example in answering the question as to whether a situation will escalate or de-escalate. In fact, the interaction is the most interesting level because it is here that you can influence the progress of the conversation. It is in this area that your influence lies: your performance co-determines what happens.

	The playing field	The other person
-1 resistance	• You feel pressured to have the other person accept something. • You are in one way or another dependent on the other person, for example because you need their permission or approval, and you have no power over them. • You must advise or persuade the other person. • It is a case of persuading someone under pressure.	• The other person is distrustful of you. • The other person feels manipulated or pressured. • The other person fears the consequences of the decision they have to make. • The other person has the feeling that their interests are not taken into account, which puts them on their guard. • The other person is not (yet) open to being influenced.
-2 emotion	• The other person is angry or disappointed about something to do with you, the organization you represent or the products you deliver. • The other person's animosity towards you is greater when the cause is rooted in something which you did or neglected to do. In which case, it may be that they hold you responsible for their anger.	• The other person has the feeling they are being treated unfairly. • There is an unexpected turn in the conversation. • Some of the other person's expectations are not fulfilled. • The other person experiences disappointment, frustration or anger.
-3 hidden opposition and manipulation	• The balance of power is unequal and has a serious effect on the situation. • If the relationship between you and the other person is long-term, mutual negative images can cause hidden opposition and influence. • Often, the other person wants something from you on this level (in contrast to level -1, where you want something from the other person). • There is little trust and openness between the parties involved.	• The other person does not see you as an equal: you are either dominant or submissive. • The other person is experiencing distrust or powerlessness; they have the feeling that your interests are widely divergent and they have to trick you to get what they want. • The other person's perception of you is not positive, which prevents open communication.
-4 aggression	• The other person sees you as representing an impregnable position. • The other person sees you as a representative of evil, for example the embodiment of the inaccessible institution they need something from and will not get.	• The other person experiences intense dependency and powerlessness and sees you as inaccessible and possibly as arrogant. • The other person has the feeling they are being treated unfairly or victimized – and they refuse this feeling. • The other person is in such a state that you cannot reason with them. • The other person sees you as an obstacle to what they need and therefore views you as the enemy.

Yourself
• You are too wrapped up in your own situation. • You want to go too fast. • You are thinking too little about the interests of the other person, or you are thinking for them. • You see the other person as a means to an end, rather than as a goal. • You have trouble knowing when to stop persuading.
• The other person's expectations or agreements made with them have not been fulfilled. • You avoided difficult issues and neglected confronting the other person about them. • You have hurt or short-changed the other person. • You do not have sufficient empathy. • You are too busy with the emotions of the other person, to their discontent. There is a big chance that you provoke certain emotions in the other person if you are not open to their feelings (in contrast to level -1, where you do not open yourself enough to the interests of the other person. In the first case you inspire distrust, in the second, animosity.)
• You are not using normal, above board influence techniques. • You are insecure and fearful or proud and arrogant; it is important to you what the other person thinks of you. • You are afraid of the other person's negative opinions. • You have difficulty with clarity. • You have difficulty making contact with your own feelings which can lead you to be trapped by indirect influence, without you being aware of this.
• You use your power and have no interest in what the other person needs. • You are not looking for a mutually beneficial solution. • You yourself become aggressive. • You have difficulty with limits, you have little self-control. • Your fear of aggression incites aggression.

Table 1 Indications of condition forming levels in a conversation, per level of learning

7

Level -4: aggression

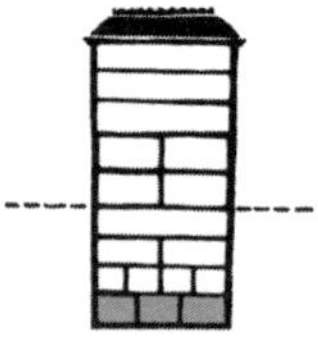

The most stressful situations arise in conversations when one of the parties involved exhibits aggressive behaviour. We are dealing with the lowest level of the winning dialogue system here. In a situation like this it is impossible to conduct a productive conversation. That means that the moment you notice aggressive behaviour on the part of your conversation partner, you have to stop whatever else you are doing immediately and focus your attention on the aggressive behaviour itself. Only once your conversation partner has calmed down can you carefully continue your original conversation.

Forms of aggression

There are three types of challenges on level -4, depending on the form of aggression:

- Aggression due to powerlessness (level -4A)
- Intimidation (level -4B)
- Physical violence or a direct threat (level -4C)

Aggression due to powerlessness

Aggression due to powerlessness usually occurs when people come into contact with institutions they are dependent on, such as hospitals or welfare institutions. Officials who can impose sanctions (police officers, traffic wardens or tax inspectors) also have to deal with aggression due to powerlessness. The way you react generally enables you to mitigate and reduce aggression based on a feeling of powerlessness. In the next chapter this will be explained in greater detail.

Intimidation

Intimidation is a variant of emotional manipulation (level -3D), where fear is used to make the other person more submissive. This form of aggression often operates under the surface and is therefore difficult to recognize; at first, the aggressor can seem very friendly. You will find more information about this hidden form of aggression in chapter 9.

Physical violence

As soon as threats of, or direct physical violence come into play, a normal conversation absolutely cannot take place. You can begin by indicating your limits, but my advice to you in this type of situation is to break off the conversation immediately. If a conversation gets completely out of hand anyway, then we are beyond the range of this book. The only aim left is the prevention of violence. Avoid a direct confrontation and do not attempt any heroics, try to end the situation and get away as quickly as possible. A few tips:

- Keep breathing!
- Make eye contact with your attacker.
- Say and do as little as possible.
- Try and keep physical distance between you and your attacker.
- Move and speak quietly and only when necessary.
- Work passively with the aggressor to avoid outbursts of violence.
- Do not take any risks to protect material goods.

Learning from aggression

The themes that go with aggression are 'control', 'calmness' and 'firmness'. Control of your own reaction is important because every situation involving aggression is provocative; a fight or flight reaction may be your first response. In most cases, it is a good idea to suppress these primary reactions because you can achieve much more with a controlled response. Setting limits works much better than answering aggression with aggression and quietly walking away is often better than an uncontrolled attempt to escape. Along the same lines, calmness is also important to ensure that you do not act out of panic because you can endanger yourself or others. An effective remedy against aggressive behaviour is a firm, quiet reaction. That helps the other person come to their senses so that you can continue speaking calmly with them.

If you are dealing with aggressive behaviour, the feelings you have are often strong and uncomfortable. The best way to handle such a situation is to stay in touch with your own feelings. The feelings that you experience in such situations are vital signals which help you to find the right words and the right tone. Sometimes these signals do not appear, possibly because you are not in touch with these types of feelings. For one reason or another, you close down emotionally in the face of aggression and therefore do not receive any signals that should help warn you of aggression. If you are open to it, I would suggest that you look into the root cause of this phenomenon.

It is also possible that these feelings link up to other situations you experienced earlier in your life, which means you receive incorrect signals. In the wave of emotion that comes over you, it is very difficult to identify emotions that are associated with the specific situation and to connect these with appropriate behaviour. You run the risk of overreacting, which causes the situation to escalate. You are, after all, reacting to much more than what is actually happening at that moment.

In both cases, your most important beacon and navigation instrument is not functioning at an optimal level, which makes your reactions stiff and ineffective. You can practice skills and learn tricks to make up for this shortcoming, but that will never work as well because your best course of action is really getting to know your own feelings. For instance, if you only know what you ought to have said in hindsight, take the opportunity to learn something about yourself. Take the time to investigate how your emotional life operates in this area if you have the idea that your emotions give you insufficient signals or take over completely.

If you are dealing with aggressive conversation partners, it can be very confrontational. But what does it mean? If you come across aggression more often than others, what does that say about you? Does your own behaviour maybe incite aggression? If you come across as aggressive or even very submissive, then that is certainly a possibility. And also if you often make use of power associated with your position or function, then you can incite others to aggression. They feel powerless and frustrated because you or your organisation decided their fate. An arrogant or distant attitude can enrage people who need something from you and do not get it.

8

Level -4A: aggression due to powerlessness

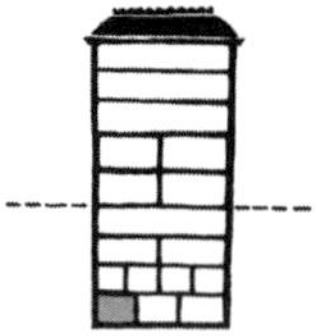

In conversations, aggression usually enters the scene as a consequence of a feeling of powerlessness and frustration. People can become aggressive when they have the feeling that their interests are being adversely affected, without their being able to do anything about it. Staff members of social services and parking services can encounter people who start a conversation aggressively. People can also get very wound up before making a complaint in shops or in hospitals, which causes them to exhibit aggressive behaviour from the outset. Aggression then takes on forms such as swearing, personal attacks and conditional threats: 'If you do not remove the wheel clamp now, I'll give you hell!' Their feeling of powerlessness over the situation provokes people to insult the other person in order to feel better. Because of their position of authority, hospital staff, police and other professionals pay the price for symbolizing the injustice that a person feels is being done to them. In that way, they try to influence the situation somewhat and obtain some degree of recompense.

The manner in which you respond to this form of aggression greatly influences the aggressive feelings of the other person. You are in a position – as long as you can keep your emotions in check – to remove a substantial portion of this aggression. This is a typical example of the enormous power you can imbue your performance with, simply by dealing wisely with the other person's feelings.

Practical tips

If you encounter aggression due to powerlessness, you may benefit from the following suggestions about how to respond:

- Be prepared for aggression.
- Remain calm.
- Give the other person's emotions some space.
- Show that you are making an effort.
- Offer clear choices.
- Speak – if possible – in terms of advantages and the interests of the other person.
- Set limits.
- Break off the conversation if necessary.

Be prepared for aggression

If you expect your conversation partner will act aggressively from the outset, then you can prepare for that. What might they be worried about? What frustrates them the most? Put yourself in their shoes, try to feel understanding. Start the conversation calmly and try to hold on to that calmness – no matter how hard it may be – throughout the conversation. Do not let the aggression get to you and unleash an (emotional) reaction! Ensure that you have your behaviour under control; do not stimulate aggression in the other person. If you are scared, you will appear to be the underdog, and if you allow yourself to react in anger, you run the risk that you (also) start to show aggression.

Remain calm

Experience teaches that aggression due to powerlessness often escalates if you throw oil on the fire, for example, by swearing back, expressing negative opinions about the other person or not taking the other person seriously. On the other hand, it appears that it is not difficult to remove this form of aggression by indicating in a controlled tone that the attack is of no use to you and that from your perspective it does not help solve the problem at hand. The advice is then: remain calm. Your behaviour can exercise a great deal of influence on the behaviour of your conversation partner. If you react calmly, then there is a greater chance that the other person will also become calmer.

Give the other person's emotions some space

By listening, by giving the other person your undivided attention and not defending yourself or justifying your behaviour, by articulating what you observe and by exhibiting understanding for their feelings, you give your conversation partner the feeling that they are being heard and understood. That gives them the chance to let off some steam, with the result that their aggression dissipates.

Show that you are making an effort

If you give aggressive conversation partners the idea that you are doing everything in your power to help them, then they will see that as positive. The fact that you are making an effort to help – even if your opportunities to do so are somewhat limited – gives them the feeling that you are conscious of their position and their aggression towards you will be substantially reduced if not completely removed. Tell them what you are going to do to help, and if possible, go the extra mile; that way you give them the feeling that they are being helped within the limits of what is possible. Do not hide behind rules and regulations and send out proactive rather than passive signals!

An example:

After a difficult delivery, a young set of new parents were told that mother and child would have to leave the hospital within the next twelve hours – those were, after all the hospital regulations. The father began to panic: the post-natal care agency was maxed out to the point that there was no help available and he did not think he could care for his wife and child on his own. He began to rant at the nurse on duty. The reaction of the nurse could be: 'I understand that this is difficult for you. I will check if it is possible for your wife and baby to stay a little longer.' If that is not possible, then she could soften the blow by showing her willingness to make an effort: 'I understand your situation, but I am afraid you will have to return home. I will do my utmost to see that post-natal care picks up where we leave off. Should there be any problems while you are alone, then you can contact this department by phone, any time of day or night.'

Offer clear choices

The less influence you allow the other person to have on the course and outcome of the conversation, the more they will feel an imbalance of power and the more likely they will be to resort to aggression. By presenting them with different choices, you give them the feeling that they can influence things, which will reduce their anger. Experience teaches that in responding to aggression, it is better to offer people choices within certain parameters. That way you not only reduce their aggression; they will also be more at ease with their choice because they were aware of the alternatives and turned them down.

An example:

A single mother has broken her big toe. Normally, the toe would be quickly splinted and put in a cast, after which a walking plaster would be applied. That would mean that the mother would be completely dependent on others in the running of her household – and when this sinks in, she refuses the treatment in an aggressive manner. She screams and threatens and drives the hospital staff to desperation. In consultation with the doctor and plasterer it is decided to let the woman choose between a walking plaster (deviating from the standard procedure) or to wait. They explain to her that a walking plaster does involve some risks, but as long as she does not overtax her foot the first few days, it is a good option to consider.

Speak in terms of advantages and the interests of the other person
By indicating why certain things happen or are being done and what the advantage of that is to the other person, you give them the feeling that the situation they are angry about is that way for a good reason. Try to speak in terms such as: 'we will do this, so that...'

An example:
'I understand that this step is very difficult for you and you see it as an unnecessary obstacle. Still, there are several examples from the past where things went awry for you financially. This guardianship is meant to smooth the financial waters for you.'

Set limits
With an aggressive conversation partner, it is important to specify what is possible and what is not. Set your limits in a calm fashion and only break off the conversation when there is no other option. But be careful with setting clear cut limits too soon! It is entirely possible that, contrary to your expectation, the other person has resolved to be a more constructive participant over the course of the conversation. In that case, it would be a shame to spoil things. Give your conversation partner the chance to pleasantly surprise you!

Break off the conversation if necessary
If it just gets too crazy for you, you can inform the other person that you will only continue the conversation under certain conditions. You threaten to break off the conversation if the aggressive behaviour does not stop. If the other person ignores your warning, you can make good your word and cut off the conversation. Be resolute, for example by standing up and walking away.

Exactly where the limits are differs from person to person. It helps to think about your limits beforehand so that you are ready to act as soon as it looks as if they may be breached. It is also good to consider

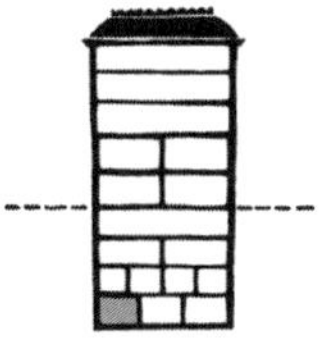

what the consequences of your action may be. By cutting off the conversation, you will most likely increase your conversation partner's frustration, rather than decrease it. Besides, there is the risk that the conversation will follow the same pattern at any other moment. As long as you are able to continue listening to the other person's story without risk of violence to yourself, then it is wise to do so. Try to filter out the other person's actual problem and address that.

If a conversation is broken off, then it is a good idea to find out if it is possible to approach the other person within a few days and discover if you can pick up where you left off. If you personally cannot do so, then maybe you can ask an intermediary such as a colleague or a manager for assistance. The advantage here is that you can clear up the problem before it repeats itself – or escalates.

Examples

Examples of ways to bring the other person back to the issue at hand:

- 'I hear what you are saying, but this is about the TV being broken, right?'
- 'Should we look at how we can solve this problem?'
- 'What happened exactly?'
- 'What exactly is it that you want?'

Examples of continuing under certain conditions:

- 'If you continue to swear at me, you prevent me from looking into your problem.'
- 'Please stop the insults, then maybe I can be of some help.'
- 'If you continue on in this way, then I will put a stop to this conversation. If you want to continue, then it will have to be without swearing.'

Examples of breaking off a conversation:

- 'Maybe it would be better to continue this conversation later, once we have cooled off a bit.'
- 'We cannot continue in this manner. I am putting a stop to this conversation.'
- 'I am going to break off this conversation now.'

Next steps

If you succeed in turning the tide of aggression, you will still have to deal with emotions, complaints and possibly criticism. Keep listening and take responsibility if necessary: maybe you yourself could have done things differently?

If your organization causes people problems unnecessarily, it is important to discuss this with colleagues and managers. Preventing (avoidable) aggression is always better!

9

Level -4B: intimidation

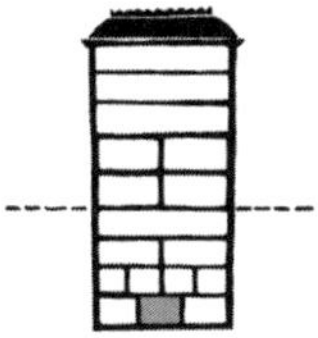

Manipulating with fear through direct or indirect threats – intimidation – comes in all shapes and sizes. In dealing with this, the focus of the winning dialogue system is on hidden or indirect threats in a conversation which are used to limit your freedom of choice and to make you more accommodating by playing to your fears.

Negative emotional manipulation (level -3D) plays into feelings of insecurity, doubt and dependence while intimidation is based on feelings of fear. In fact, intimidation is the aggressive variant of emotional manipulation: 'I could of course have a little chat with your boss', and: 'you know I'm a nice guy, but don't make me angry...'

Contrary to aggression due to powerlessness, this form of aggression is usually used in a premeditated and purposeful way by someone trying to get what he wants. There are even individuals and groups who consciously build up a reputation for intimidation. If members of a motorcycle gang or a group of rowdy teenagers show up on the scene, they do not have to say a lot to strike fear into the hearts of those present.

If you are not aware of it, intimidation can be a source of very strong emotions and fierce counter reactions. A distinct characteristic of intimidation is the apparent calm and friendliness with which it is employed, a reason why this form of manipulation is so difficult to recognize. That friendly face is not at all in accordance with the agenda behind the aggressor's message. To prevent intimidation getting a hold of you, it is important to realize what is going on. As soon as you are aware of what the other person is trying to do, his unfair attempt to influence you unawares has failed.

Practical tips

It is better not to respond at all than to buy into the intimidation with a fearful reaction. In the latter case, the aggressor knows for certain that he has you where he wants you. Ignoring intimidating remarks can also be seen as a sign of weakness by the other person, or even as an invitation for him to step it up a bit. A cool response is therefore preferable, for example: 'This isn't getting us anywhere. Shall we discuss the business at hand?', or: 'Sorry, but I really can't do anything with this. I think it's better if we talk about something else.' Make sure however that you do not overreact or make the mistake of becoming aggressive yourself.

An alternative is to ask what your conversation partner means to say exactly. Intimidation loses much of its force if someone has to clearly explain what they actually mean to say. Should you not be able to put a stop to the intimidation this way, then you can try to bait them by asking directly if they are making a threat. This response is very to the point and shows that you are not scared.

If you are un-nerved by the intimidation, you can indicate that you do not wish to discuss things further under this type of pressure. That way you can try and negotiate your way out of an intimidating situation. Examples of this include:

- 'I will examine your arm, but I am not doing anything until your friends have left the premises.'
- 'I cannot do anything for you as long as you stand here shouting. If you take a seat, I will explain the possibilities.'

By indicating your willingness to help or cooperate depending on a cessation of the intimidating behaviour, you show the aggressor that that behaviour is in fact blocking progress. If you can make him see that the only way to proceed is to stop using intimidation, more often than not he will give up his attempt.

Examples

Examples of intimidation:

- 'You know I am a nice guy, sweet to my Mum, but don't make me angry.'
- 'If we do not reach an agreement, I won't be responsible for the consequences.'
- 'I really do not know what will happen if you tell John Smith about this, but I would make certain you are far away from me. '

Examples of setting limits on intimidation:

- 'We are not getting anywhere like this. Let's look at the problem.'
- 'I suggest that we resolve our problem rather than examine the ultimate consequences.'
- 'Well, I am feeling very pressured. Is that what you want?'

Examples of continued questioning:

- 'What exactly do you mean?'
- 'Do you mean that last remark as a threat?'
- 'Is it your intention to threaten me?'

Next steps

A cool reaction presents the other person with a problem: how can they continue dealing with you? It can help if you encourage them in a mature, calm and sympathetic manner to resolve the situation in discussion. There is a chance that the other person will become emotional after an attempt at intimidation, after all, the trick did not work. Let the emotions come. You probably have no desire to deal with anger and emotion, but anything is better than an intimidating conversation partner.

10

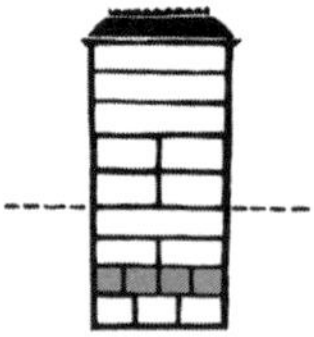

Level -3: hidden opposition and manipulation

The various challenges on level -3 all have one thing in common: the real problem is not clearly visible. Whereas on levels -4 (aggression), -2 (emotion) and -1 (resistance) you can quickly get an idea of what is going on with your conversation partner just by being a good listener, the problem on level -3 is less superficial. This mysterious aspect is part of the challenge on this level. In order to face the challenge, contact with your feelings is even more important than on the other condition forming levels.

Causes of hidden opposition and manipulation

On level -3, the system distinguishes four challenges:

- Lack of commitment (level -3A)
- Negative opinions about you (level -3B)
- Negative behaviour (level -3C)
- Emotional manipulation (level -3D)

Lack of commitment (level -3A)

A lack of commitment is usually evident at the beginning of a conversation, but it can also become clear only when it is time to close an important deal. What it comes down to is that your conversation partner is taking part in the conversation, but in fact is (not) yet ready to have the conversation and deal with the resulting consequences. Signs of a lack of commitment in the other person are lethargy, passivity, disinterest or explicit reluctance. Arriving too late, being unprepared or having forgotten important documents are also signals along the same lines. You can read about how to deal with an uncommitted conversation partner in the next chapter.

Negative opinions about you (level -3B)

Negative opinions about you may stem from your history with the other person, from stories about you that are making the rounds or from negative conceptions about your profession. These mainly present a problem at the beginning of a conversation; in general, over the course of the conversation, they give way to the experiences built up in the conversation.

You can recognize negative opinions about you in behaviour exhibiting distrust, fear or contempt. Your conversation partner may come across as distant, formal or careful – as someone who does not really relish the idea of doing business with you. In some cases, they may try to make their opinions clear to you through verbal or non-verbal hints. You can read about how to deal with this in chapter 12.

Negative behaviour (level -3C)

During the conversations you conduct, you can be confronted at any moment with obstructive behaviour from you conversation partner. Obstructive behaviour comes in all shapes and sizes and of course depends on your own opinions, feelings and limits. You might be frustrated in situations where your conversation partner continuously interrupts you, contradicts you, belittles you or disregards the agreements made about the structure of the conversation. The question of how to handle obstructive behaviour is up to you. Read about how you can determine what to do in chapter 13.

Emotional manipulation (level -3D)

This unfair attempt at influence usually arises during negotiations or situations involving persuasion. Your conversation partner uses techniques designed to play on your feelings in order to make you malleable or increase your willingness to make concessions. Emotional manipulation is very common, in varying degrees. In many cases, conversation partners manipulate each other without being aware of what is going on. In order to arm yourself against emotional manipulation it is important to develop a sharpened awareness. Read more in chapter 14.

Learning from hidden opposition and manipulation

Influence versus manipulation

In reality, influencing another person is the aim of many forms of communication. In and of itself, there is nothing wrong with this, but it becomes manipulative the moment someone gives you the feeling that you are being denied something essential: your freedom of choice not to accept their influence. Manipulation more or less stands for consciously eliminating choices by influencing feelings of inferiority, dependence or insecurity, with the goal of reducing another person's capacity to exercise their free will. As soon as you feel pressured, you can speak of manipulation. Manipulation is compelling – someone takes the space rather than earning it – and this happens in an underhanded (surreptitious) manner.

Influencing another person is a process in which, even in the most extreme situations, choices are always available. With influence, the other person has earned the right to influence you in your process of choosing. You receive help in the form of information about your decision making process in order to make it easier or faster. In this way, your conversation partner still completely respects your freedom of choice.

The difference between manipulation and influence is therefore primarily a question of denying or limiting another person's freedom of choice. In short, influence is a desire and manipulation is a (often hidden) demand.

Sensitivity, courage and strength

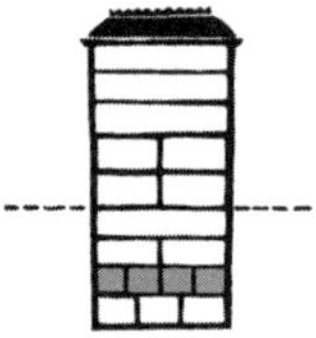

The themes that go with hidden opposition and influence are 'sensitivity', 'courage' and 'strength'. In order to identify the nature of a hidden agenda, you must be in close contact with your feelings; to understand what is going on you have to trust your intuition. You need courage to bring up the problem and strength to face the unwanted influence or to do what is necessary to get a commitment or alter negative opinions.

If you have difficulty with the challenges on this conversation level, you can ask yourself if you take the signals your feelings are giving you seriously. Many people receive these signals, but dismiss them as unimportant or avoid them for the sake of convenience. Other people immediately associate a reaction, an opinion or another feeling with the original feeling without pausing to reflect on the feeling itself. In the latter, usually unconscious process, often lies the reason why emotional manipulation works. If this is the case with you, you can try to re-establish contact with your feelings and examine them one by one, so that you learn the difference between your feelings in a situation and the unconscious conclusions you associate with them.

With negative behaviour, as with emotional manipulation, it can be important to shed light on the situation quickly. Because if you allow your frustration to build up for too long, the eventual confrontation will be laden with more emotion than the specific situation would normally warrant, which prevents the conversation from being constructive. You need courage to discuss your dissatisfaction in a timely manner, especially if there is an imbalance of power to your disadvantage. If you notice that this is difficult for you, then analyze what the alternatives are. Ultimately, a careful confrontation is always to your advantage. If you have a lot of trouble with this, you may ask yourself why you hesitate to bring clarity into an unclear situation.

For problems with commitment and negative opinions about you, you need the strength to step up to the other person, especially if the situation is tense and you yourself are having difficulty with (the performance of) your conversation partner. Try to develop the ability not to feel dependent on the opinions of others, and learn to obtain your self esteem from within yourself and not from your contact with others. That makes you much less susceptible to every form of hidden influence and opposition. If you feel strongly dependent on the approval or acknowledgement of others, that may be an interesting theme to explore in your own personal development.

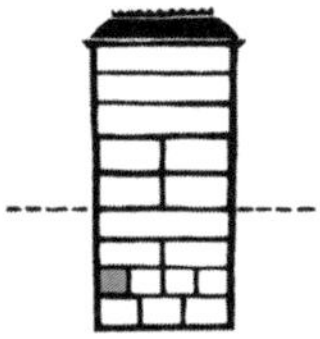

11

Level -3A:

lack of commitment

Undoubtedly, at some point you have landed in a situation where it seems that you just could not get any further with your conversation partner. There was no connection. They responded listlessly or indifferently, made irritating comments or did not come to the point. Or even worse: sometimes they didn't react at all. They were not focused and acted passively. All of these situations are examples of insufficient commitment, in which your conversation partner has no desire (anymore) to have a conversation with you. Most of the time, this attitude can be traced back to the fact that the other person needs acknowledgement of a problem, an issue or a certain emotion that they are dealing with.

Practical tips

If you want a commitment from someone who feels strongly about a certain issue, then you will have to bridge the gap with a good deal of acknowledgement from your side. Even if you feel badly treated and short-changed and are also in need of some validation, it is important to first acknowledge the feelings of the other person. The art of receiving validation (and commitment) is being the first to give it.

In most cases you can prepare for a lack of commitment by thinking beforehand about the possible negative feelings your conversation partner may have and the causes of these feelings. During the conversation try to get the other person to talk about what is bothering them. Put yourself in their shoes and try to express their feelings in words, without including your (ideas about those) feelings. There is a big chance that you are not on the right track and that can lead to strong emotions on the part of your conversation partner.

In general, people will appreciate your efforts to view the situation from their perspective. Be patient and see how far you come without exercising a lot of pressure. Besides, a lack of commitment almost never arises spontaneously: usually something has happened to bring it about. Examine your own role in the situation critically, be prepared to take responsibility for your part and do not avoid any old sores in doing so!

Commitment is a condition to moving forward; it does not do any good to continue a conversation when your conversation partner is participating with half of their attention or less. If you cannot foster any commitment, you must ask yourself if it is worthwhile to continue. Maybe you are not the right person for the job?

Examples

Examples of acknowledging the other person's situation:

- 'I can imagine that you have no desire to talk after everything that has happened to you.'
- 'I understand that you feel very badly treated.'
- 'We are here of course to discuss the conditions for the sale of your house, but may I first express my sympathy for the situation you find yourself in?'
- 'I can imagine that it is a big disappointment to have to have another discussion when you thought the case was already closed.'

Next steps

A lack of commitment is often the outermost layer of something deeper: emotion. If you have reached the point that you can approach the emotions of the other person, you will notice that they have a story to tell. About what depends on the situation, but in any case, be prepared to be confronted with intense emotions. After you have given your conversation partner the necessary acknowledgement and the lack of commitment has been transformed into involvement, you can (usually) continue on to level -2 (emotion).

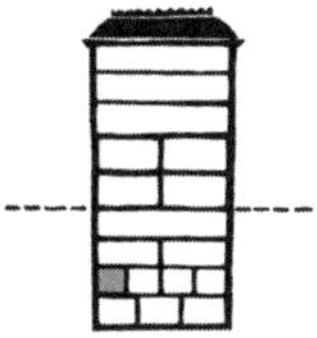

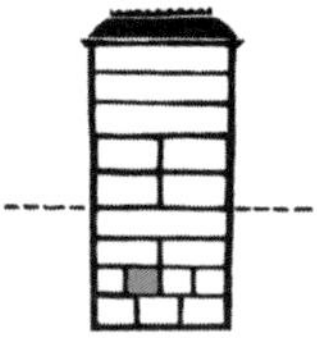

12

Level -3B:

negative opinions about you

You may have experienced a conversation partner who had such strong negative images about you or your intentions that it was nearly impossible to have a good conversation with them. It turned out that they (mis)judged you to be an enemy or competitor, or had the feeling that you were impossibly proud, inaccessible or arrogant. If you feel this type of resistance and try even harder to achieve your goals, you will run into a brick wall. Try as you might to dance around these negative images, before you can begin having a constructive conversation, you will have to confront these images head on. The influence of the negative images on your conversation is so great that you have to overcome this barrier as quickly as possible.

I am assuming here that the negative images of the other person are at the very least partly incorrect and that you are prepared to change behaviours that the other person feels are disturbing.

Practical tips

In order to remove negative feelings about you or your intentions, you first have to make it clear that you suspect that the other person has negative images about you. Describe what you observe and ask if your conclusions are correct. If the other person confirms that they feel that your intentions or behaviour is disturbing, then the ball is in your court and it is up to you to either act or accept the consequences. Try to clarify the situation by expressing your good intentions. Do not get defensive, but show some understanding of the other person's feelings and indicate that you are willing to change your behaviour.

Avoid the pitfall of claiming that your behaviour was a reaction to the other person's behaviour. It is not that simple and if you use that line of reasoning, you run the risk of encountering more conflict. You are in fact passing responsibility for your behaviour onto the other person. If you think about it, you will see that you always have a choice in how you behave – regardless of the other person's behaviour.

Examples

Examples of ways to bring up negative images:

- 'I would first like to apologize for what happened during our last conversation. I get the impression that you were rather shocked, is that true?'
- 'I have the feeling that in this case you see me as your enemy, is that correct?'
- 'Do you have the idea that I want to railroad you?'
- 'It seems as though you think I am playing a game here. Is that true?'
- 'It is not my intention to play a trick on you.'
- 'I am looking for a solution we can both live with.'
- 'I would like to discuss the situation in a calm manner, so that we know how to handle these types of issues in the future.'
- 'I am absolutely not out to take advantage of my position.'

Next steps

If you approach the other person in this way, it will have an enormously positive effect on the conversation. Of course your words must be put into action, so make sure that you put your positive intentions into practice and abandon any vengeful behaviour. Often, your conversation partner will react to what you say and the interaction can lead to a chance to continue the conversation. Hopefully the barriers can be crossed much more easily now. Should your attempt to de-escalate the situation fail, try to reach a number of agreements to make the conversation workable. And if your conversation partner's images are so strong that you do not succeed in removing the negativity, then you can ask yourself if it is worthwhile continuing – or if you need assistance from a third party, a mediator, for example.

13

Level -3C: negative behaviour

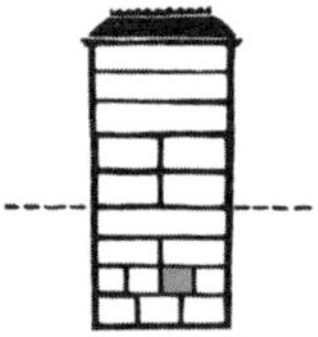

If you notice that your conversation is threatening to derail or if the behaviour of your conversation partner is starting to irritate you, then it is time to take corrective action. More or less hidden negative behaviour is caused in general by the fact that your conversation partner, for one reason or another, is not interested in (parts of) the conversation.

For example, if you are working on resolving a conflict, ulterior motives may be playing a role. It is possible that the other person is not yet ready to settle differences. In that case, you both have different expectations of the conversation, which pretty much ensures that it will grind to a halt. Even if you feel that the other person is dominating or unpleasant, it can lead to resistance from their side.

Because this resistance does not usually play out on the surface of the conversation, it can be difficult to do anything about it. The result of this is that your irritation increases and the risk of the situation escalating grows greater. For this reason it is important to nip negative behaviour in the bud. It is a serious mistake to continue a conversation even though you feel there is something fundamentally wrong. Additionally, not only do you endanger your relationship with the other person, it will probably be impossible for you to achieve a satisfactory result.

If you tend to ignore resistance you have observed or if you find it difficult to talk about, this may be rooted in various reasons. Try to be aware of the inner resistance and see if you can manage to avoid it. Realize that your conflict evading behaviour can have the exact opposite effect. A discussion about negative behaviour can be very valuable as it enables you both to address your mutual annoyances so they can be resolved. The moment you do this is determined by your own sense of the situation. As soon as you get irritated or notice that you are looking at your conversation partner in a more negative light, then it is time to make this the subject of the conversation. Another reason to have a time out is if the conversation has stalled. If you are repeating things for a third and fourth time, you can rightfully doubt the efficacy of the discussion.

Practical tips

Speaking about the conversation in its own right –communication about the communication – is known as *meta-communication.* You interrupt the ongoing conversation and its content in order to discuss the form in which you are communicating with one another. Make sure that you do not allow your irritation to determine the tone of this process – in doing so, you may come across as too intense which will only worsen the situation. Be aware that people who are unfamiliar with meta-communication can view it as threatening. Partly because of this the way in which you speak is very important: if your tone is dominant or pedantic and confirms the fears of the other person, your attempt at meta-communication will not yield significant results. Discuss your experience calmly and indicate what you think is going wrong with the communication in clear, neutral words. The best way to do this is to describe what you think both of you are doing, without pointing a finger at your conversation partner. Besides a concrete description of the behaviour you are observing, try to explain what you feel the consequences are and what effect it has on you. In doing so, you can refer to your own emotions, the effectiveness of the conversation or a result that you have noticed. It helps if you do not present your opinion of the conversation in general terms, but as a statement about how you feel. By confronting the other person only with your personal opinion and not with a blanket statement, your message comes across in a less threatening and pedantic way. For the rest: communicating what you feel and experience does

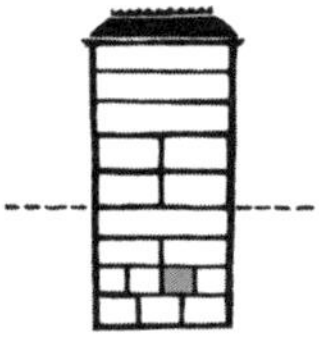

not necessarily mean that you cannot ask the other person to give an explanation for their negative behaviour.

Do not forget, once you have had your say, to find out what your conversation partner's opinion is and where they think the difficulties lie. It is possible that they do not see your point or start to act defensively. Try to listen and emphasize, if necessary, that you are having trouble with the way in which the conversation is progressing.

It is possible that your conversation partner has trouble with the way you are conducting the conversation. Allow them to express their dissatisfaction and learn from it. Try not to go on the defensive, but be willing to learn and act constructively. In most cases, you will see that meta-communication immediately improves your contact with the other person and the quality of the communication. You end up on the same level so to speak, and then continue on from where you left off. In order to avoid falling back into the same situation, you may want to make agreements with each other before you actually pick up the conversation again.

Meta-communication is a serious intervention in a conversation and is not entirely without risks to your relationship with the other person. Use this corrective method therefore only when other, less intense interventions are not working. Before you go into meta-communication ask yourself if something simpler might also work. For example you could take a break for coffee, ask a few interested questions, or change the subject.

Examples

Meta-communication in a conversation:

- 'Mary, I think we need to stop for a minute. I have the impression that we are hurling insults rather than looking for a solution. I think we are not going to get anywhere like this. What do you think?'

- 'Mr. Johnson, before I explain my proposal once again, I would like to say that I don't think you agree with my suggestions for improvements. I get the feeling that you do not take my ideas seriously. Am I mistaken?'

Meta-communication in a group:
'I am interrupting the training here because I would like to address something. I notice that people are not really listening to each other's presentations. The result is that presenters lose their concentration and this detracts from the learning process. What is going on?'

Next steps

In order to prevent drifting away from your original conversation, do not take too much time for meta-communication. Try to absorb the feedback you get and continue where you left off with the necessary constructive information.

14

Level -3D: emotional manipulation

Emotional manipulation is misusing emotion in order to influence another person's feelings so that they are more likely to give into concessions that professionally they otherwise would not. Exhibiting emotion can be a powerful means of manipulation, in order to provoke sympathy or inhibit the progress of a conversation (Mastenbroek, 2004). Should you suspect that your conversation partner is using emotions to manipulate you, then it is imperative that you discuss this without giving credibility to their emotional position.

Positive and negative emotional manipulation

There are two types of emotional manipulation: positive and negative.

Positive emotional manipulation

With positive emotional manipulation, the other person tries to make you more accommodating by arousing positive feelings of care, responsibility, sympathy or dependence. Examples of positive emotional manipulation include giving compliments or expressing appreciation (you are rewarded), acting helplessly (so that you have the feeling that you can assist) and flattery. If you are sensitive to smooth talk, if you do not like disappointing people, if you have a strong sense of responsibility or if you tend to want to rescue weaker individuals, then be on your guard for positive emotional manipulation.

Examples of positive emotional manipulation:

- 'I have so much admiration for your precision. What you are capable of is so valuable. I wish I was so precise – especially now that I have to turn in my manuscript in a week...'
- 'Oh no. It can't be true. I cannot believe this. I really do not know what to do. I am at my wits end.'
- 'You are of great value to this organization. Your loyalty has been seen and noted. I trust that you will not let us all down in this case.'

Negative emotional manipulation

Negative emotional manipulation is intended to arouse negative feelings in order to make someone more accommodating. With this form of manipulation, the other person wants to play to your feelings of doubt, insecurity and dependence. Ironic remarks, questions about qualifications or experience, expressing impatience and making fun of others are all tried and tested strategies. If you end up in a situation where your insecurity may influence you, then watch out for negative manipulation!

Examples of negative emotional manipulation:

- 'It's not a big deal that you failed; after all, you are still young and inexperienced.'
- 'Can you fill in for me today? Or does that make you a little nervous?'
- 'Okay, so this is the best we can expect from you today?'
- 'Well, thank you kindly for your new offer. But I have the idea that we come from different planets. How long have you been a real estate agent anyway?'
- 'I would do my very best on the piece if I were you since Carl always picks apart sloppy work and we cannot exactly say that you are little miss perfect, right?'

- 'I don't want to come across as impatient, but is there a chance that we could get a response on our proposal today?'

Practical tips

In order to understand how to deal with emotional manipulation, there are three things you need to know. Firstly: despite the fact that emotional manipulation is meant to influence your decisions unfairly, it is a common way of interacting with others which we have learned to use to get our way from our youngest years. Do not therefore be angry or disappointed if you catch someone using emotional manipulation; people often use it without thinking.

Secondly: emotional manipulation is most harsh when it is hidden. The most painful manipulation is a word or gesture which is specifically aimed at your weakest points. The better people know you, the better able they are to manipulate you. It is important that you recognize emotional manipulation (or an attempt at it). The degree to which you are aware of the fact that you are being manipulated determines how effectively you can deal with it. That is why it is so important to stay in touch with your feelings during a conversation. If you become irritated for unexplained reasons, start feeling insecure or pressured, there is a big chance that you are being manipulated. The more you are aware of your feelings during a conversation, the less likely it will be that you know how to respond only in hindsight.

Thirdly: once you know you are being manipulated emotionally, its effectiveness largely evaporates. You do not always have to react actively to manipulation. If you wish to do so and confront your manipulator with their behaviour, it is important to do so carefully. The risk of escalation is great. Some tips to reduce that risk as much as possible include:

- Stay in touch with your feelings.
- Do not make concessions under pressure, especially emotional pressure.

- Do not buy into the manipulation.
- Reject the manipulation – without unnecessarily damaging the relationship – by going back to the topic of conversation.
- Interrupt the conversation if necessary should your conversation partner continue manipulating you and identify the behaviour and the effect it has on you (meta-communication, see previous chapter).
- Watch out for feelings of superiority due to positive manipulation – or feelings of inferiority and dependence in the case of negative manipulation. They stand in the way of clear thinking.
- With negative emotional manipulation you can probe a hidden negative remark.

Examples

Examples of ways in which you can confront negative emotional manipulation:

- 'Isn't it better to limit ourselves to sharing out the tasks?'
- 'I understand your rush and irritation, but let's deal with things one by one.'
- 'I suggest that we not focus on the number of years of service, but on the business we have to do together.'
- 'I don't see how this is bringing us closer to a solution. Shall we look at your previous proposition again?'

Asking questions for clarification can be a good way to let the other person know that you are aware of the fact that you are being manipulated. Manipulation loses the best part of its power when it is no longer concealed:

- 'What exactly do you want to say?'
- 'You just said that you had a rough time with our district manager.

What do you mean by that?'
- 'How should I interpret you drumming your fingers?'

With positive emotional manipulation, the common advice is not to buy into the emotional behaviour. React indifferently and bring the focus back to the essence of the conversation. You might try the following responses:

- 'I think it's great that you value my friendship, but let's talk about costs.'
- 'I understand that you are dependent on my permission, but in this case I have to represent more than one person's interests.'
- 'Thanks for the compliment. Shall we continue?'
- 'What other topics do we have to discuss, besides the sensitive subjects that you are talking about?'

Next steps

Manipulation usually stops once your conversation partner sees from your reaction that nothing will come of it. You can choose to manoeuvre around it, or to subtly let the other person know that you know what they are up to. Afterwards, you can continue with the conversation level where you left off. Should the other person persist in manipulation, then continue to try and correct the conversation and bring up the behaviour and its effects. You will find more information about this in chapter 20.

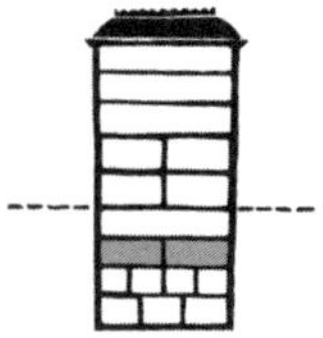

15

Level -2: emotion

Emotional behaviour

Shouting or crying, a long silence or a flood of arguments, unreasonable demands or accusations – all of these are expressions of emotion. You may be faced with these in a confrontation and you will have to do something about it. As long as your conversation partner remains over emotional, they are not capable of discussing things rationally or logically which makes it terribly hard – if not impossible – to achieve your professional goals.

If you know beforehand that your conversation partner is angry or sad, you can take that into account right from the beginning of your conversation. It becomes more complicated if emotions break loose over the course of the conversation, in reaction to bad news for example. The emotions can be directed at you, your behaviour or the organization you represent, but can also be brought about by something completely unrelated to you.

Criticism and complaints

Sometimes complaints and criticism go hand in hand with emotion. If your conversation partner makes negative remarks about you, your behaviour, your product, your colleague or your organization, it can create a stressful situation for both parties. This is partly why many people keep their complaints or criticism to themselves at first, and only bring them up when, from their perspective, things get really out of hand. That means that it is entirely possible that if you are confronted with criticism or complaints that your conversation partner is already irritated. They will then use emotions to cross an imaginary threshold and confront you with what is bothering them. In that case, there is a big chance that the emotions are intense and not proportional to what you might have expected from the current situation.

The difference between emotion (level -2), manipulation (level -3) and aggression (level -4)

In practice, it can be quite tricky to distinguish emotion from aggression, especially when it is aggression due to powerlessness. The difference between aggression and emotional behaviour lies in the aim of each: aggression is mostly meant to force you into something, while emotional behaviour – as harsh and intimidating as it may be – is not used intentionally. An emotional conversation partner is looking for understanding and a listening ear. The aggressive person demands action, and now, or else... If you are not sure if you are dealing with aggression or emotion in a specific situation, then you can assume that it is emotion. If you are dealing with an aggressive conversation partner, you will know soon enough.

You can also distinguish between emotion and emotional manipulation in this manner. Manipulation is purposeful and functional, while emotion just is what it is.

Practical tips

If you are dealing with an emotional person, the most important thing is to control your own emotions. Because you may get the feeling that you are being attacked, you may tend to try and defend yourself or your organization. The worst thing that can happen is that you yourself become emotional, which will probably cause the situation to escalate. Two people who have difficulty being reasonable together have limited chances of ever finding a solution. To be sure, a situation involving two emotional people will not escalate as quickly if they have a close relationship, such as partners, friends or colleagues whose underlying bond will ensure that they eventually come together again. Often, a really good argument can clear the air.

People who are feeling emotional do not get anything from a rational discussion. If you begin a conversation with someone who is in an emotional state, do not start off with your opener or another constructive suggestion because your emotional partner wants to talk about their problems, and preferably as soon as possible. Most emotional conversation partners are in need of understanding and acknowledgement. Allow them the space to express their emotions. If you let your conversation partner let off steam you give them the chance to shake that weight off their shoulders. Show them that you take their feelings seriously, for example by clearly saying that you understand the situation. And try to put yourself in their shoes: how would you feel if you were in their position?

You can give an emotional person the best acknowledgement by identifying their emotions or summing up, a technique also known as *reflecting feelings*. In doing so, you identify the emotions underlying what the other person has said in a way that is as accurate and sincere as possible. In reflecting feelings, you filter the other person's message for emotional elements and repeat these back.

Example:
'How is it possible that you have not delivered what I asked for four times in a row? I am furious! Is that clear?! Are you paying attention when I am talking to you?'
'Yes, I can hear that you are really angry!'

Another effective way to calm down an emotional conversation partner is to articulate what emotions you observe. You can do this by saying for example: 'I see you are looking puzzled', or: 'I notice your face becoming tense', which shows the other person that you are aware that what you are doing or saying is affecting them in one way or another.

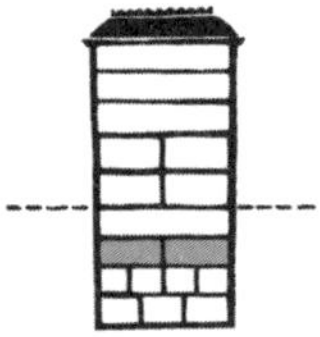

By identifying the behaviour you observe you give the other person an opportunity to respond – and confirm whether or not your hunches are correct. Make sure that in doing so you do not interrupt your conversation partner but listen with your full attention so that they can vent their emotions. At first, be careful not to ask too many questions and so encourage the other person to go into (greater) detail. Do not ask them to divulge more than they want to. By doing so, you often achieve the opposite: rather than telling you more, the other person may clam up. In dealing with emotions, it is important that you distinguish between expressing understanding and expressing agreement. As long as you express understanding, you treat the emotion appropriately: with attention and without opinion. If you react to the content of the emotion while your conversation partner is emotional, you invite them to mix content and emotion and that can lead to difficult situations. That is part of emotional manipulation or specific forms of aggression, as discussed in previous chapters.

In situations where emotion plays a role, it is important to keep in touch with your feelings. As soon as you notice that the emotion is too intense for you or you feel that you are being pressured to make a decision based on emotions, a suspicion that more than emotions are involved may be justified.

It is possible that your conversation partner was hurt in a conflict with someone else and is involving you in one way or another. Based on your reaction, they will categorize you as a friend or an enemy. Friends are socialized with and enemies are fought with. In order to avoid becoming involved in the conflict, it is critically important in such a situation that you stick to understanding and acknowledgement without expressing an opinion.

Examples

Examples which can help you respond to emotion:

- 'I can see that it touches you.'

- 'I notice that you are disappointed about it.'
- 'I hear that you had expected something different in that area.'
- 'I can imagine that you...'
- 'If I were in your shoes, I would feel the same thing.'

To personal criticism:

- 'You think I should have approached things differently?'
- 'You are dissatisfied with the progress of my project?'
- 'I am very sorry that you had so much trouble.'

To complaints:

- 'That is of course not the intention.'
- 'I understand that our XXP is not functioning as it should.'
- 'I hear how many problems you have had with our products.'
- 'Thank you for coming back.'

Next steps

If your conversation partner calms down after a while, you can listen more actively and ask questions about what happened. Depending on the type of answers you get, you can assess their emotional state. If you get calm answers of substance, then you can carefully continue to the next step. If that goes well, you can soon resume a reasonable conversation.

Difficulty dealing with emotion?

Themes that go with dealing with emotions are 'empathy', 'understanding' and 'being open to the other person, without taking over their emotions'. If you can apply these reactions in the right doses,

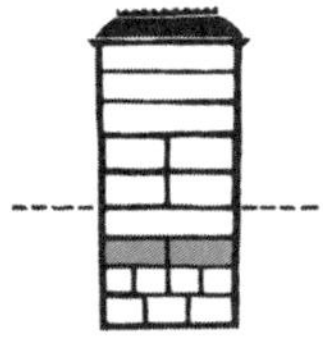

you provide your conversation partner with an opportunity to express their emotions and be heard, understood and acknowledged. That way, you enable them to calm down. Your focus on the other person does entail one risk: by being so concentrated on the other person you run the risk of losing sight of the relationship between your feelings, your situation, your interests and those of your partner. That is why you must stay alert and never lose sight of your side of the story!

A number of important pitfalls to remember when dealing with an emotional conversation partner are:

- Getting wrapped up in the intense emotion and becoming more accommodating in the hope that the other person will calm down faster
- Becoming emotional yourself
- Ignoring the emotion
- Crying too
- Expecting the other person not to be emotional: 'Calm down,' or: 'Be reasonable for once'
- Agreeing with the other person (with the result that you are stuck)
- Disagreeing with the other person (with the result that you become the enemy)
- Being pedantic
- Defending yourself, making justifications or blaming the other person

Your own emotions are too strong

If you are confronted with another person's emotions, it is possible that your own emotions make it difficult for you to react in an effective manner. It is also possible that you freeze up and lose touch with your emotions. Your own emotions are so intense that you cannot or will not be confronted with them. In both cases, your emotions have a great deal of influence on your behaviour and limit your ability to deal with the emotions of the other person. Do you feel attacked or threatened by your conversation partner's emotions? Is it against the rules according to you to show emotion and therefore is the other person doing something that you would not allow yourself to do? If you have answered this or both questions affirmatively, it can help to focus on your own feelings. By examining them, you can get more insight into your emotions and ways in which you can separate yourself from other people's emotions.

Do you incite a lot of emotion?

There are various reasons why some people incite more emotional reactions than other people, or do so more frequently. A few of these are:

- If you focus too little attention on the interests of others or allow situations which short-change others to continue, it can lead to unsatisfied expectations, disappointment and frustration.
- A blunt, closed or hurtful attitude leads to sadness and anger in others.
- If you often allow yourself to be influenced by emotions, other people might misuse that by playing on your emotions to get you to do things.
- Shirking your responsibilities or necessary confrontations with yourself or with others can lead to exasperation in people who work with you or are dependent on your work.

If you notice that you are dealing with emotional people more frequently than other people, you can assume that there is something about you that provokes emotion, or at least stimulates it. It might be helpful to take a look at this. If you succeed in finding the cause and can increase your awareness it can be an important step in increasing the effectiveness of your contact with others. Ask someone you trust how you come across and ask yourself where your behaviour comes from. Your behaviour is probably being influenced by images and it would be more than worthwhile searching yourself and find out where these images come from.

16

Level -1: resistance

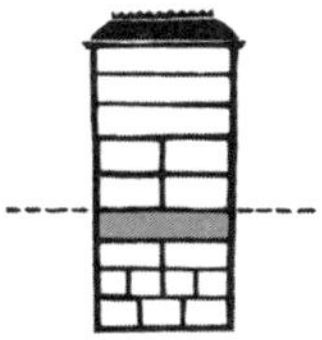

Resistance is an expression of a lack of acceptance of you personally or of what you are saying. Especially in situations where you are trying to persuade someone or change something, resistance is a common reaction. This is how your conversation partner is feeling: they are not (yet) prepared to accept your plans, ideas or suggestions.

Resistance can be expressed in varying degrees. It is possible that at first you are not at all aware of any resistance from your conversation partner. But the fact that you do not notice any resistance does not mean that it isn't there! If you want to do something about this resistance, you have to start by bringing it to the fore. Openly expressing objections is the most explicit form of resistance. Objections to your ideas are most common in situations where you are trying to advise or persuade others without having any power over them. In commercial situations, objections as an expression of resistance also occur regularly.

You can recognize resistance in the other person's tendency to react indifferently or negatively to your argument or proposal. The reaction: 'Yes, but...' is very obvious, but resistance can of course be expressed less explicitly. If you are giving advice or trying to persuade someone, be aware that every flat or indifferent reaction can point to resistance.

If your conversation partner reacts negatively to you in one way or another, it does not necessarily have to be a problem. Resistance indicates involvement. And if you deal with it properly, it definitely does not have to be disadvantageous: objections are perfect opportunities to discuss crucial information. Information which you can use to your advantage: you can adjust your proposal accordingly, better inform your conversation partner and persuade them in an effective manner of the merit of your idea.

Practical tips

Dealing with resistance is not easy. The most important reason for this is that your negative, uncomfortable feelings and those of your conversation partner reinforce one another, which makes it unclear as to where the source of the resistance is. People exhibiting resistance often feel uncomfortable. They are not satisfied with a proposal or are not entirely convinced of the advantages. Maybe they do not see enough of themselves in it or they do not (yet) feel sufficiently acknowledged. Maybe they are scared of the consequences of your message or have a problem with your approach to the conversation. The timing can be a difficulty with this last point: someone who has to accept a new idea will readily see you as too driven. That is why you can usually see resistance as a 'stop signal.'

If you need to persuade someone, there is always something at stake. A project that must be approved, a reorganization your conversation partner has to see the use of or a creative solution which has to be accepted make situations involving persuasion stressful. If you feel resistance from your conversation partner, stopping is the last thing that you want. Even worse: there is a big chance that you feel bad about not being able to convince the other person. At moments like this your emotions can get the better of you. The idea that your goals seem farther away than ever can lead to you being impatient, irritated or frustrated and give you the feeling that something has to happen quickly to turn the tide. As a reaction to resistance, the tendency to put more effort into persuasion often arises, in the hope that by doing so you can reach the desired result. But the opposite is true: this increased effort only brings you farther away from your goal. The conversation partner who was not open to your ideas will only see further persuasion as very annoying. Their stop signal was not heeded by you and worse, there is still too little acknowledgement, reassurance or deceleration from you! As a result of this, they will develop more resistance to the initial idea and to you as the originator and messenger. That leads to more frustration on your side – and with that, the circle is complete. Many good initiatives die a premature death due to this spiral of resistance, which again, you can easily recognize by the fact that both parties are continually saying 'Yes, but...' to each other at various intervals in the conversation. It will be no surprise that such conversations generally do not amount to much.

Concerns of the persuader	**Concerns of the other person**
'I will probably not be able to persuade her'	'I will let myself be persuaded easily and will definitely not be overwhelmed!'
'I have spent a lot of time on this proposal'	'Have my interests sufficiently been taken into account?'
'It is very important that I close this deal'	'Can I trust this person?'

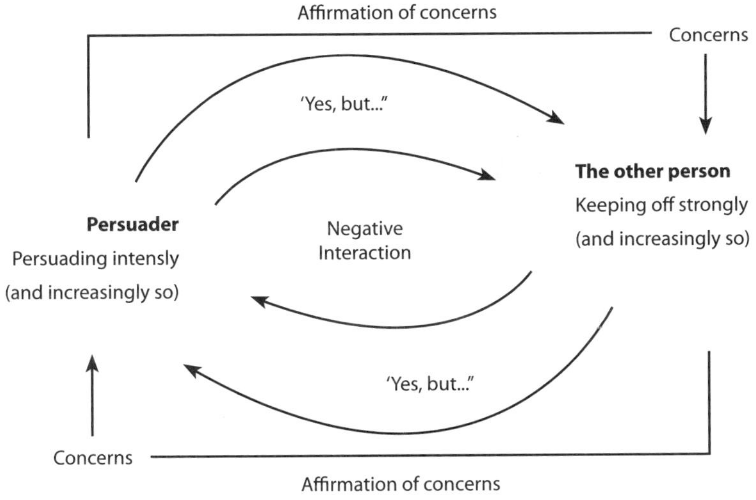

Figure 1 The negative spiral of resistance

Procedure

Dealing effectively with resistance requires that you break the negative spiral. Rather than fighting against the resistance, you recognize the objection of the other person and work with it. This procedure entails five steps:

1. Sense
2. Encourage
3. Clarify
4. Acknowledge
5. Respond

Sense

The sooner you notice resistance, the smaller the chance that you will end up in a negative spiral – and the bigger the chance that you can do something about the resistance. That is why developing an antennae for resistance may be the most important way to learn how to deal with it effectively. For example, if you are persuading someone, it is beneficial to keep an eye on your conversation partner's non-verbal behaviour. Another good way to quickly identify resistance is to stay in contact with yourself: if you feel the pressure mounting during a conversation and you start trying to convince the other person more energetically, be on the lookout for signs of resistance. As soon as your conversation partner does not let you finish speaking or reacts with 'Yes, but...' you can assume that you are dealing with resistance. That is the moment to abandon the conversation level you were at and to switch to level -1 (resistance).

Encourage

If you suspect that your conversation partner is resisting, it is important to interrupt your argument and give them space to make objections. You are then in fact heeding the stop signal and switching from talking to listening. This indicates to your conversation partner that you

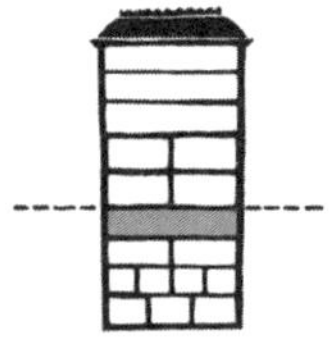

do not want to get stuck in the negative spiral and you are prepared to take their resistance seriously. It is in your best interest to make the resistance explicit because you cannot do anything with hidden resistance. Therefore encourage your conversation partner verbally and non-verbally to go into their objections in more detail. But be cautious! Experience teaches us that asking pointed questions in response to an objection can be seen as threatening by the other person. You have to encourage your conversation partner in a careful manner, for example by telling them that you understand their perspective then summing up their objection and asking for elaboration. If you notice resistance purely based on physical signs, you can identify the behaviour and ask for an explanation. Finally, there is another important distinction: do not forget that encouragement is different from agreement!

Clarify

Try by asking questions to get a clear picture of the resistance and keep in mind that you can only deal with specific objections. Sometimes people are not ready to express their true objections and use other protestations as a smokescreen. By continuing to ask questions you can get behind that smokescreen and figure out what the real resistance consists of. In doing so, the type of questions you ask and the intention with which you ask them determines your success. If you ask confrontational questions, you actually end up back in the spiral of resistance. In order to really get a handle on the resistance, your questions must stem from involvement and a desire to really understand your conversation partner. Ensure that you get all the relevant information; do not stop questioning until you think you understand the resistance completely. It is important to really know what the sticking points are, otherwise you cannot react effectively.

Acknowledge

In order to be sure that you have understood the other person correctly, it is a good idea to summarize the objection in your own words and check to see if you summary is a good one. A good summary proves that you have put yourself in your conversation partner's position and acknowledged what they said. Only once they have the feeling that you take their resistance seriously enough will they be prepared to listen to your side of the story. By expressing involvement and interest, you earn the right as it were to continue on to the next step (responding). Your summary is a natural platform for a continuation of the conversation.

Respond

If you have gone through the previous steps with good results, you have earned the right to explain (again) your point of view to your conversation partner. You can pick up the role you temporarily put down to listen to the other person and continue with the conversation level you were at. It is now critical to take into account, to whatever extent is possible, what you heard while dealing with the resistance. The better you handle your conversation partner's real worries, the greater your chance of achieving your goals in the conversation.

At first, it can feel unnatural to deal with resistance in this manner, but I can assure you it is worth the effort.

Examples

Example of a situation involving persuasion with a negative spiral:

A: 'If this organization wants to compete in the market, then they will have to invest in new technology.'

B: 'But our current machines have not yet been written off.'

A: 'The point is that the competition is much farther along: the market demands renewal.'

B: 'Yes, but the cost price is then under pressure.'

A: 'But that problem will only affect you in the future.'

B: 'Well, then we will have to solve this in the future as well.'

Example of this situation without a negative spiral:

A: 'If this organization wants to compete in the market, then they will have to invest in new technology.'

B: 'But our current machines have not yet been written off.'

A: 'Do you see this as an obstacle to renewal?'

B: 'Well, not exactly an obstacle, but it would be a shame not to utilize the investment to its full extent.'

A: 'When will the existing machines be written off?'

B: 'Let me check, the last one in about three years.'

A: 'What other obstacles do you see?'

B: 'Well, the average age of our people is rather high. Renewal may be difficult for many of them.'

A: 'So because of the write off, it would be desirable to continue working with the current equipment for another three years. And furthermore, you expect some resistance from your employees.'

B: 'Yes that's it.'

A: 'Okay, given the developments with your competitors your market position might be jeopardized if you do not invest in renewal in the short term. And to overcome the problem of adjustment for your staff you might consider starting on a small scale. In that way your organization could learn and adjust gradually. Then once your equipment has been written off, you could switch completely to the new technology.'

Example of a situation involving persuasion with a negative spiral:

A: 'Due to your high cholesterol and blood pressure, I urgently advise you to lose some weight.'

B: 'Yes, of course, but I have tried over and over again. It just doesn't work.'

A: 'It is a question of discipline. You know what they say about a moment on the lips...'

B: 'Yes, I hear it in my dreams.'

A: 'Well, you have to decide for yourself. I can prescribe a medication to help out, but ultimately it is up to you to do the work.'
B: 'Okay, I will do my best.'

Example of this situation without a negative spiral:
A: 'Due to your high cholesterol and blood pressure, I urgently advise you to lose some weight.'
B: 'Yes, of course, but I have tried over and over again. It just doesn't work.'
A: 'What happens then?'
B: 'Oh, it goes well for a while, but then I gain more weight than I lost.'
A: 'Are you talking about the yoyo effect?'
B: 'Exactly. I know I have to change my lifestyle, but it's hard for me.'
A: 'What is keeping you from doing so?'
B: 'I don't think I know enough about the options. I often eat out and if I am at home I eat something readymade. I don't know what I have to watch out for.'
A: 'What I hear you saying is that you want to lose weight, but you haven't had any advice that works for you and leads to long term weight loss.'
B: 'Yes, that's right.'
A: 'There are lots of ways to help you. Shall I send you to an experienced dietician who can advise you about some effective programs?'
B: 'Yes, that seems like a good idea. Thanks so much.'

Next steps

If you have dealt with the resistance successfully, return to the interaction level you were at and pick up the conversation again. You run the greatest risk of encountering resistance when you are trying to persuade your conversation partner, but also when presenting the structure of the conversation or during negotiations resistance can come up.

If in a specific conversation you fail to deal successfully with your conversation partner's resistance, you could make another attempt and keep questioning until you know exactly how they view the situation. If you have the idea that you cannot get a handle on the resistance, other issues may play a role; in which case it can help to talk about your observations.

Difficulty dealing with resistance?

The themes that go with dealing effectively with resistance are 'patience', 'care' and 'healthy curiosity'. Patience is necessary because your resistant conversation partner is not interested in your schedule or in the goals you are trying to reach. Care is necessary in order to place your conversation partner's interests in the foreground and focus on helping them. You can use your curiosity to get to the bottom of the situation and the interests of the other person.

If you notice that you often meet resistance, is may be useful to find out why. The sources of resistance are often the same as the causes of difficulties resolving the resistance. Particularly if it is in your interest to convince your conversation partner (quickly) there are plenty of dangers to watch for. The most common and most important of these I will address below.

Too soon

It is possible that you are just presenting your advice to the other person too soon. This might be because you spent (too) little time listening to their interests and perspective before you started trying to persuade them. Another possibility is that you have not built up enough credibility or trust with your conversation partner. Try to answer the following questions: Why am I in such a hurry? Is it my own impatience or do I feel the need to offer more resistance to people or other factors that put pressure on me?

Your interests or those of another?

It is also possible that another person does not see their interests represented in your proposal. Even if you think that you understand your conversation partner's perspective, it is still possible that you did not identify their situation and their interests when you presented your idea. If your reasoning is based on your own perspective and your own interests, it usually inspires resistance. People do not allow themselves to be persuaded easily if they have the feeling that they are being used for another person's purpose. If this is true for you, then you need to realize that your success is determined by other people and it is therefore more than worthwhile to understand what their motives are.

Being open to resistance

If you deliver a presentation or explain a proposal passionately, often you are not really open to negative feedback from your surroundings. That causes you to notice resistance too late or not at all. And then it can happen that, before you switch over to the resistance level, you are already trapped in the negative spiral of resistance and you have a lot of catching up to do. The misconception that there is nothing wrong as long as you don't hear anything can be at the root of this problem. Do not switch off your own feelings; stay alert for signals that can point to resistance!

Personal style

Sometimes your personal way of persuading does not appeal to your conversation partner. Which can inspire resistance –they thinks you are too dominant, aggressive, or too careful or too slow. If your personal style inspires resistance, you can examine how you can perform in a more generally accepted manner – without harming yourself of course.

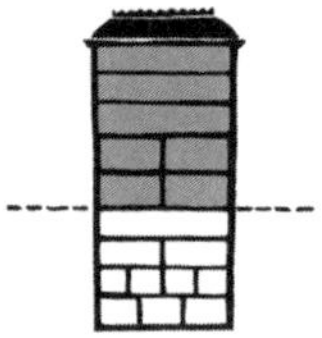

17

The constructive conversation levels

Contrary to the condition forming levels, on the constructive conversation levels, you can achieve concrete professional results. In the winning dialogue system these levels are ordered in a way that you can conduct a logical and solidly built conversation. The different constructive levels can successively yield the following results:

Level 0: introducing structure

On this level – either at the beginning or over the course of the conversation – you introduce the order of the topics you wish to address. It forces you to think about the subjects to be discussed and helps you to structure your conversation beforehand. Furthermore, it is a useful guide for the conversation which you can fall back on if necessary. The zero level of the winning dialogue system is central in the following three chapters.

Level +1: exchanging information

On level +1 you receive information from your conversation partner and in return you give them (in most instances) your information. This conversation level applies to a large number of conversation situations which are discussed in chapters 21 through 25.

Level +2: value adding negotiations/problem solving

The benefit arising from this level is that the results of the negotiation are advantageous to both parties based on your interests and those of your conversation partner. By thoroughly exploring these interests – and especially the weight that you and your conversation partner wish to give them – you can increase the room for negotiating as much as possible, which helps you achieve a win-win solution. After the more general negotiation techniques covered in chapters 26 through 28, chapter 29 goes into specifics regarding value adding negotiations and problem solving.

Level +3: value sharing negotiations

If you do not succeed in merging your interests with those of your conversation partner on level +2, you can still reach your goals on the interaction level above that by looking at possible concessions you or the other person could make. In contrast to value adding negotiations, your focus here is sharing the value which is being negotiated. Value sharing negotiations are addressed in chapter 30.

Level +4: wrapping up and closing deals

The result of this conversation level is a completed conversation where what you have been discussing is summarized to the satisfaction of you both and agreements made are confirmed. You can read more about this in chapter 31.

18

Level 0: introducing structure

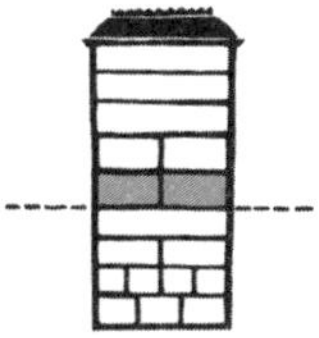

Introducing structure is important, especially in professional conversations. Most people underestimate the importance of this step, and skip it, thereby missing a powerful aid in achieving their desired purpose. In the winning dialogue system, introducing structure occupies a special place – that of the 'ground floor,' level 0. This level works, as it were, as a transition between the condition forming (underground) and the constructive (above ground) conversation levels.

You can see introducing structure as a condition forming level and therefore as part of the underground levels. On the other hand, coming to an agreement about the agenda or subsequent steps is a first concrete step forward, which would make you likely to categorize it as one of the constructive levels of the building. However you see it, the zero level is always the starting point of a constructive conversation, unless your conversation partner becomes emotional or aggressive. Also during a conversation, in certain situations, it can be necessary to pause and reflect on the structure of your conversation. You can read about this in chapter 20.

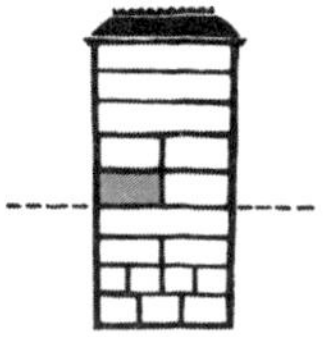

19

Level 0A:

The conversation opening

The most constructive, respectful, professional conversations begin with an agreement about structure and content. Agreement about the topics and the order in which you will discuss them co-determines the effectiveness of the conversation and can also positively influence the tone. A good conversation opening, in which you focus on and allow space for the other person's position and interests, shows your conversation partner your interest in finding a mutually beneficial solution. Tip: by addressing the points which most worry the other person early on, you increase the chance that they will accept your proposal.

If a conversation does not appear to be hampered by emotional or other obstructive elements, it is a good idea to start with an opening so that you can synchronize your expectations with those of your conversation partner. In effect, you are asking them to go along with the form of conversation you are suggesting. This is an important moment because you can influence what will be discussed and in what sequence. That is why it is wise to take the lead and come up with your own suggestion.

It is possible that there is some tension about the content of the conversation or that there is some emotion involved. In these situations, it is better to prioritize the emotional issues above the structure and address these sensitive subjects first. For example, if a client has a complaint about your product, your conversation will go much more smoothly if you first give them the opportunity to express their dissatisfaction and then discuss the structure of the conversation. In this example therefore, you do not begin immediately with the opening, but introduce structure at a later stage by means of an intermediate procedure proposal. The following chapter goes into this in more detail.

The former is in fact nothing more than a specific application of the underlying idea of the winning dialogue system: address lower levels before you begin with the higher levels.

Practical tips

If there is no reason to delay, you can begin the conversation with a short, informal introduction aimed at breaking the ice, followed by an opening. A conversation opening consists of four parts, which are explained below:

1. The reason
2. The agenda
3. The benefit
4. The control question

The reason for the conversation

To be certain that the reason for the conversation is clear to your conversation partner, give a short introduction answering the question: 'Why are we meeting today?'

The agenda: what will be discussed?

Next, identify the subjects you feel need to be addressed and the order in which you wish to discuss them. In effect, you are answering the question: 'What am I planning?' Tip: when establishing your agenda, take into account the (supposed) interests of the other person. By showing your insight into and interest in the points they probably want to cover, you make it easier for yourself to make the conversation a success. You can also impose a time limit when discussing the agenda. Thanks to this agenda, your conversation partner will know what to expect from the conversation.

The benefit: how does your conversation partner profit from your suggested approach?
In order to clarify the points on your agenda and to convince the other person of their merit, it is important to lay out the benefits of your agenda. By means of this explanation you establish a connection between your suggested agenda and the results you want to reach together with your conversation partner. With a good explanation, you show your involvement in the interests of your conversation partner and you provide motivation for the conversation. You answer the question: 'Why should you spend your time on this?'

The control question: is the other person in agreement with your suggested approach?
By asking the other person if they feel comfortable with the agenda proposal once you have made it, you involve them in the agenda. They can immediately agree or suggest changes and extra points. If they agree to your proposal, your opening has become an outline of the conversation sanctioned by both you and your conversation partner. That means that both of you can refer back to it at moments when there is a digression in the conversation. It is then no longer a one sided proposal made by you. If you do not ask the other person about their opinion during this phase, then you give them the opportunity to back pedal and not really get involved. A positive response to a control question ensures an active participant.

A common mistake made by conversation partners in the opening phase of a conversation is that they get into the content of the conversation too quickly. The effect of this is that there is no explicit consensus reached about the agenda of the conversation. The consequence of this is that both conversation partners can have divergent expectations and there is a greater possibility of confusion at a later stage. Even with subsequent conversations it is a good idea to make a well structured opening, including a short summary of what was discussed in earlier conversations. That way, you ensure that you are immediately on the same page as the other person. Other than that, it is useful to ask if anything has changed since the last conversation. This can prevent a number of misunderstandings and unpleasant surprises!

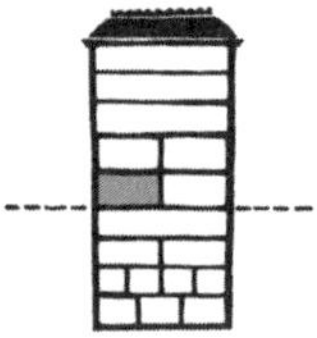

Examples

Account manager speaking with a client:
'Mr. Johnson, we agreed to look once again at new archiving solutions for your organization. I suggest that we first discuss your situation and your needs. Afterwards, I can show you a number of solutions so that you can decide which solution would work best for you. Do you feel comfortable with this approach?'

Manager conversing with a staff member:
'Mary, we are having this conversation with regard to your upcoming maternity leave. I suggest that we first address wrapping up and handing over your responsibilities. After that I would like to look at the period after your leave. That way we can finish everything off and clarify everyone's expectations. Okay?'

Doctor in consultation with a patient:
'After examining you over the last few weeks, we know what's going on with your hip. There are several different possibilities for treatment that I would like to discuss with you so that we can decide which would be best for you. Do you agree?'

Political negotiation:
'After our last meeting, we still had some differences of opinion. I suggest that we first look at our common interests. Maybe from that

point of view it will be easier to find agreement. What do you think of that idea?'

Next steps

If the other person accepts your proposal, you can continue the conversation with the first point on the agenda. If the other person objects to your proposal, you first have to address the suggested agenda. It is possible that your conversation partner has other ideas about the further course of the conversation. In that case, you can discuss his ideas for how the conversation should continue and then try and merge both of your ideas to come up with a new structure. If there is more going on, such as emotion or distrust, then it is a good idea to switch back to the appropriate conversation level and work through those feelings before moving on. Continuing with the content of the conversation without there being an agreement between the two conversation partners about the agenda is a waste of time: without his involvement, the conversation will yield unsatisfactory or no results. Finally this: keep the procedure in mind during the conversation so that you can refer back to agreements made should you or your conversation partner digress.

Difficulty with the conversation opening?

If you have difficulty structuring conversations, it is usually due to one of the following factors:

- Your position in relation to your conversation partner
- Your personality
- Your overview
- Your discipline

Your position in relation to your conversation partner

It is possible that in a certain situation you do not feel you are in a position to exercise influence on the course of the conversation, for example because you are in a relatively junior position. If you can trust the other person to conduct the conversation in a manner satisfactory to you, then you do not have to act. But, if you are unsatisfied about the course of the conversation, or have reason to doubt a positive outcome, then you are short-changing yourself and the other person if you do not indicate this. Tip: if you have to pull yourself together to defend your position, then make sure that you do not come across as too forceful or inflexible. Present your suggestion calmly and if necessary discuss the further course of the conversation with your conversation partner.

Your personality

Not only your position, but also your personality can make it difficult for you to structure the conversation beforehand in discussion with the other person. For example, if you are too submissive or have trouble taking the initiative, you may have difficulty standing up for your ideas. In general, that does not have to be a problem as long as you speak up; if your conversation partner respects you, they will listen and taken notice of your wishes.

Your overview

If you have no idea of what you want or can't plan a logical course for the conversation, it can be next to impossible to make a convincing conversation proposal. If you often have difficulty gaining an overview of the situation, good preparation is extra important for you. The winning dialogue system can help you with that: by going through the levels, you can solidify your goals. As you gain more experience with the system, you will be in a better position to see the most desirable course of a conversation before you start it.

Your discipline

One last reason why people can have trouble with structuring a conversation is a lack of discipline. Many people cannot or will not take the trouble to prepare for a conversation, meeting, training session or conference, no matter how important their role is. If this sounds familiar, it can be worthwhile to find out the cause of this. Often, stress, nervousness or fear can be reasons why people do not want to think ahead. But avoiding structuring due to negative emotions does not solve anything. Introducing structure and taking initiative can be an excellent way of dealing with these types of obstructive feelings in a positive and proactive manner.

20

Level 0B: the intermediate procedure proposal

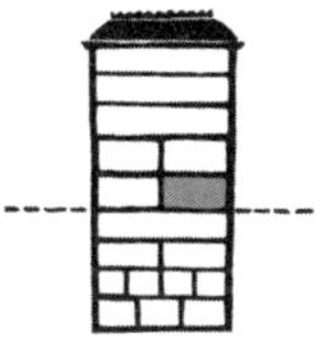

It is not only useful to introduce structure at the beginning of a conversation, but also as an intervention during a conversation. If you have come from the condition forming levels to the point where you can start working on the constructive levels, it is a good idea to make a quick pit stop at the structuring level. There is good reason for going there when moving from condition forming to constructive conversation levels. This structuring during the course of the conversation is called an intermediate procedure proposal.

There are many moments when an intermediate procedure proposal can be constructive. If you have diverged from the structure originally agreed on (for example in order to deal with emotion) and you and your conversation partner are ready to move on, an intermediate procedure proposal is very useful. It is a good way to return to the level you had been working on.

An intermediate procedure proposal is additionally useful in giving structure to a conversation where certain subjects keep coming up without being concluded. Also if you or your conversation partner cannot see the forest for the trees due to the amount of information, going back to the structure can be an effective tool.

Another moment that an intermediate procedure proposal can prove its use is if the conversation has bogged down. If you notice that your position is far removed from that of your conversation partner and you do not expect them to give way, a procedure proposal can help you to bring the conversation into more constructive waters.

Practical tips

An intermediate procedure proposal can look like the following:

1. A short summary
2. The procedure proposal
3. The control question

A short summary

You begin with a short summary of what has occurred in the conversation so far and indicate why you want to move in a different direction by means of the procedure proposal.

The procedure proposal

After you have explained your reason for a renewed structure, you make a procedure proposal for the continuation of the conversation, indicating why you feel that this direction is the most constructive.

The control question

By asking your conversation partner if they are comfortable with your proposal, you show that you are open to their opinion. After receiving approval, you can reach a consensus about your proposal. This was addressed in depth in the previous chapter.

Examples

The working of the procedure proposal can best be illustrated with examples.

An intermediate procedure proposal at the transition from lower to higher interaction levels

Manager and staff (after discussing hidden opposition):
'I'm glad we could talk about my worries for a bit. Shall we pick up again discussing my suggestions for improving efficiency?'

Lawyer and client (after establishing limits in response to aggression):
'Thank you for your apology, let's get back to work. If you tell me exactly what happened according to you and what your role was, then I will try to create an overview of your legal position. Okay?'

An intermediate procedure proposal during chaos or confusion

Account manager of a financial institution:
'I notice that we are talking about a lot of things all at once. Maybe it is a good idea if you first indicate what your wishes are in regards to your future mortgage. Then we can look at the possibilities and the consequences of each option. Does that sound like a good approach?'

An intermediate procedure proposal in a stalled meeting

Head of sales in discussion with sales managers:
'Everyone has their preferences with regard to the division of regions. I don't think we will get anywhere this way. Shall we first make an inventory of where all the sales managers live without immediately linking these with sales regions? After that we can look at how we want to divide up the tasks and the rewards. Do you think that is a good way to do this?'

Next steps

If your conversation partner goes along with your procedure proposal, you can continue with what you have agreed on. If it turns out that they have a problem with your proposal, you have to find out what that is and what your conversation partner's wishes are. Ask how they would like to see the conversation proceed and try to reach an agreement about the further course of the conversation.

Difficulty with the intermediary procedure proposal?

The hurdles that can crop up with an intermediate procedure proposal are very similar to those which can occur with an opening (see previous chapter). That means that during the conversation you have to establish the need for an intermediate procedure proposal, formulate a procedure proposal for yourself and choose an appropriate moment to present it. In some situations it can be helpful to stop the conversation for a bit in order to prepare for your procedure proposal.

Making an intermediate procedure proposal requires the well developed ability to rise above the conversation. It also requires a great deal of self-confidence, courage and forcefulness, especially if you are dealing with a dominant conversation partner. But here also: practice makes perfect. And don't forget that both you and your conversation partner have the right to determine the course of the conversation!

21

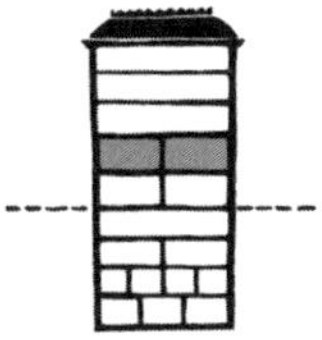

Level +1: exchanging information

The exchange of information is the first layer of the constructive portion of the winning dialogue system and is therefore the first conversation level where you can achieve concrete results with your conversation partner. In most cases, after a procedure proposal, you can begin immediately with exchanging information. Sometimes you have to take the necessary steps in the condition forming conversation levels in order to exchange information in a constructive manner. Your mutual willingness to take one another seriously and be open to what the other person has to say is of essential importance in doing so.

Result

The result of exchanging information is dependent on the topic of conversation and can vary widely from situation to situation. The big picture comes down to results in the following areas: you and your conversation partner acquire knowledge and information; you both gain (more) insight into the situation and into each other's position and intentions, which builds trust and reinforces the relationship. Ultimately, it becomes possible to exercise influence on one another.

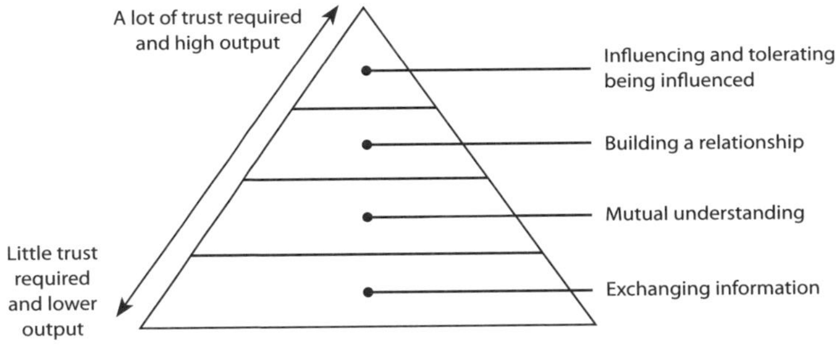

Figure 1 Depth of exchanging information

Receiving and sending

The exchange of information can be categorized into receiving information on the one hand and on the other hand, providing (or sending) information. Especially in informal conversations, this process happens naturally for the most part. In professional conversations, that may not be the case and it is wise to handle this consciously. Especially if you want to advise, influence or persuade someone, it is a good idea to remain in the listening role for what may seem a long time, and then subsequently have your say in response to what you have heard. This method of communication, in which you use the information you have received in your response is very effective. In addition to the fact that you can adjust the content of your information to suit the situation of your conversation partners, they will accept your information much more readily because they feel heard and therefore will be open to your side of the story.

The general rule for exchanging information is: first listen, then tell. Listening (receiving information) is on level +1A of the winning dialogue system, which is lower and therefore has a higher priority than giving information (level +1B1) and persuading and advising (level +1B2).

Exceptions to this rule are those situations when you already have information which provides the basis for the conversation. These include conversations involving bad news, feedback and discussion of problems. In these cases the subject itself is the motivation for the conversation and there is no reason to hear your conversation partner out first. You will find more information about these exceptions in chapter 24.

In most conversations, and namely those in which you and your conversation partner are deeply involved in the subject or if there is a lot at stake, both of you want the chance to tell your story. That can lead to neither of you listening to the other person well or sufficiently, which can lead to tension or irritation. The advice to listen more and

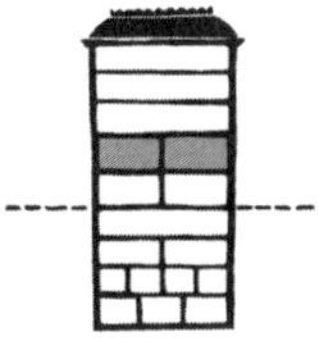

with greater attention is very valuable. But attentive listening is not the only way to exchange information effectively: the right timing, a good handle on the situation and a sharp formulation of the information also play determining roles in successfully sending information.

Providing information (level +1B)

Informing someone means transferring information in a way that is as comprehensible as possible. In fact, you want to achieve two goals with it:

- You want the message to be heard
- You want the message to be understood

And if you want to persuade your conversation partner by means of this information, then there is yet another goal: the message not only needs to be heard and understood, it also has to be accepted.

22

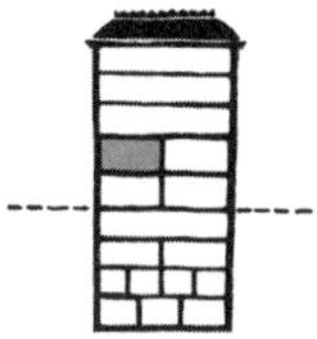

Level +1A: listening, receiving information

The reason for listening to another person is, in the first place, to obtain information. That can be general information, but it can also be information which helps you understand how your conversation partner views the situation. Listening plays a vital role in building a relationship of trust. The attention you give your conversation partner in the form of listening is often experienced as pleasant: they feel heard and understood. This is certainly true if the relationship is stressful and is therefore a useful tool in keeping the conversation on track.

Typical reasons for listening include:

- To receive information
- To gain insight into someone's situation, wants and needs so that you are in a better position to advise them at a later stage, for example as part of an advisory or sales conversation
- To build trust with the other person and give them the feeling that you take them seriously
- To give someone the opportunity to tell their side of the story after an irritating or confrontational experience
- To give an emotional person the opportunity to let off some steam, even if it is aimed at you or your organization
- To give someone the opportunity to advise or influence you

The power of listening is so great that you can also apply the techniques outlined below to the condition forming conversation levels. For example, if you give someone who is resistant a chance to tell their side of the story, they will feel that they are being taken seriously. By listening to an emotional person you allow them to let off steam. You decrease tension by visibly and attentively listening. Be open and involved so that the other person can tell their story unhindered and with a safe feeling.

Depending on the goals you are trying to accomplish by listening, you will listen in various ways. If you are primarily focused on gathering (professional) information, you will be most interested in the content of what your conversation partner tells you, while in other situations you will devote more attention to their feelings.

Perhaps you have attended a course or training in the past which addressed listening techniques, or read about them in management or sales books. Then you are familiar with the theory, but there is a big difference between knowing the theory and being able to apply it. Listening is harder than you think! The technique is complicated and, in addition to insight, demands quite a lot of practical experience. It takes time, study and practice to become a good listener in any situation. Perfect listeners are rare indeed: in my training programs I notice again and again that nearly everyone has room for improvement in this area, which in turn would benefit them directly...

Practical tips

Merely registering what your conversation partner says is often not enough because you run the risk of being informed incorrectly or incompletely. Most of the time it is necessary to encourage the other person and help them to (further) structure their thoughts. With an active manner of listening you stimulate them to give as much information as possible. The skills which are necessary to do so, both verbally and non-verbally will be addressed below.

Non-verbal listening skills

While listening, your non-verbal behaviour – what you are doing while you are listening and where no speech is involved – is of crucial importance in obtaining all the information you need. The main forms of non-verbal behavioural aspects while listening are the following:

- Eye contact
- Posture
- Affirmations
- Pauses

Keep eye contact

Eye contact is an essential sign of attention and courtesy. By regularly looking at your conversation partner while they are speaking, you stimulate them to tell their story. An associated advantage is that you will also see the non-verbal signals your conversation partner is using to reinforce the message.

If you maintain eye contact, it is important to be aware of the intensity and duration. Too much eye contact (such as staring or a penetrating gaze) can be seen by your conversation partner as threatening, which will make them less open. On the other hand, you will not reach your intended results with too little or an insufficient amount of eye contact. The right level of eye contact depends on the situation, the relationship between you and your conversation partner and your respective cultures. In order to avoid an overdose of eye contact, it is better if you do not sit or stand directly opposite your conversation partner during the conversation. This gives both of you the opportunity to look the other way from time to time so neither of you need feel uncomfortable or pressured.

Posture

A person's posture during a conversation is often an interesting source of information for the other party. The manner in which conversation partners sit or stand is a typical example of a signal that is often unconsciously sent out, received, processed and interpreted. Often, people do not realize that the body posture – that of themselves as well as that of their conversation partner – plays an important role in the commu-

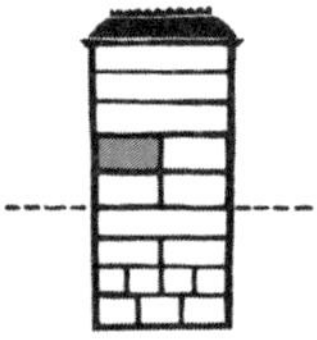

nication process. By consciously handling your own posture and actively understanding the posture signals of the other person you as a listener can actively influence the dynamics of the conversation: an interested posture stimulates the other person to tell you more.

Using affirmations

Non-verbal signals such as nodding and making listening noises have an encouraging effect on the speaker. Certainly on the telephone, (audible) affirmations are often valuable: they form one of the few opportunities to urge the other person on and confirm that you are listening. In a face to face conversation this technique has the same effect. At the right moment and with the right intonation, 'yeah' and 'mmhmm' work perfectly, though for this too the rule applies that you should not overdo it.

Make use of pauses

'Patience is a virtue', and is certainly true when creating some stillness in a conversation. Give yourself and your conversation partner the chance to collect your thoughts before moving on. Many people are prone to immediately fill the silence when another person stops speaking. That is a shame because you disturb the thought process of the speaker and stop the flow of information. Try and create some space in your conversations. Give your conversation partner enough time to finish talking and permit a certain amount of silence. Wait a few seconds before responding after they have finished. Short silences often stimulate an elaboration of the story.

Verbal listening skills

The term 'verbal skills' relates to what you say and how you say it, and includes how to ask questions in order to obtain concrete information. The main forms of verbal listening skills include:

- Open and closed questions
- The turbo question
- In-depth questioning
- Summary

Open and closed questions

Good questions – both open and closed – show interest and help you bring in-depth information to the surface. Open questions are distinguished from closed questions in that you are not putting words in the other person's mouth and do not limit the range of possible answers to the question. You give your conversation partner the opportunity to freely give information they feel is relevant. If you ask a closed question, you limit the answering possibilities for your conversation partner. Typical closed questions include:

- Yes or no questions: 'Are you satisfied?'
- Choice questions: 'Would you like coffee or tea?'

Closed questions are useful if there are a limited number of choices available, for example, in the case of control questions. But in practice, closed questions are often asked at moments when an open question would be more effective. Closed questions reveal relatively little information, mostly because they are usually the assumptions or opinions of the questioner, and can lead to uncomfortable situations, misunderstandings or damage to the relationship. That is why you should use closed questions selectively; actually only in situations where there are only two choices.

In order to become aware of your inclination to ask closed questions and then to replace them in time with open questions, you have to be able to recognize a closed question. A reminder which can help: closed questions usually begin with a verb.

Examples of closed questions (1) and an open alternative (2):

1. 'Are you having a hard time?'
2. 'How are you doing?'
1. 'Are you also happy with the new management?'
2. 'How do you feel about the new management?'

Open questions usually being with: 'how,' 'what,' 'where,' 'which,' 'to what degree,' 'in which way,' or 'why'. Tip: be cautious with the why-question as this can be seen as threatening: the other person can take the question as a criticism.

Good listeners have a focused approach: they start with general questions and keep questioning in order to gain specific information. By working with this 'lobster pot model' you follow a lightly focused and non-threatening course towards the information you are seeking, while giving the other person enough room to tell their story. With the lobster pot method, you work from broad, general information to specific issues. You are therefore working in a very structured manner: you start with a general question and then follow up with a more focused question about one of the subtopics which came up in the other person's answer ('What exactly do you like about this management, and in your opinion, what points are not so good?'). Subsequently you question further ('What do you like about this management compared with the previous one?'), then you summarize what you have heard and return to the top of the funnel in order to address another subtopic in a similar way. Once you have handled all the relevant subtopics, you can summarize and conclude (this part of) the conversation.

The turbo question

Open questions can be made even more effective by furnishing them with a 'turbo charger'. You do that by wording the question in such a way that you 'charge' it with a power that forces your conversation partner to place the subject in another frame of reference. With a turbo question you give your conversation partner a pair of glasses which enables them to see familiar issues in a different light. This creates added value for them as well: you offer them the chance to develop new insights.

Turbo questions are especially useful when the quality of the information you need from the other person is important, and in situations where trust and understanding must be built up between you and your conversation partner. Advisors and salespeople, for example, benefit hugely from turbo questions.

There are four ways to furnish a question with a turbo charger:

- Ask for a comparison
- Ask for a ranking order
- Ask for the opinion of others
- Invite speculation

Comparison

Open question	**Turbo question**
'What do you think of the results this year?'	'If you compare the results from this year with those of last year, what do you notice?'
'What advantages does this option hold for you?'	'In what respects is this option better, compared with other possibilities?'

Ranking order

Open question	**Turbo question**
'Why is it going so well with the new product line?'	'What are the two most important reasons for the success of your product line?'

'What criteria do you have for material suppliers?'	'What are the three most important criteria for selecting a material supplier?'
'What is keeping you from placing the patient on a list for a donor kidney?'	'What are the two main reasons why you do want to place the patient on a list for a donor kidney?'

Opinions of others

Open question	**Turbo question**
'What problems do you have in your department?'	'What problems would your staff most like to see resolved?'
'What do you think of the quality of information services for others?'	'What do others think of the quality of information services?'

Speculation

Open question	**Turbo question**
'What would you like to change about your staff's workplace?'	'Say that you have physical impediments, how would you arrange your staff's work place?'
'What new products would you like to add to the existing product line?'	'If there were no financial limitations, how would the product line look?'
'What logistical problems would you like to solve?'	'Say that you could suddenly change three things logistically, what would they be?'

These examples show that questions equipped with a turbo charger go deeper than normal open questions. This makes it harder for your conversation partner to answer your questions; they have to form old data and standard answers into new information and specific answers. In general, they will not find this annoying, but there are a few things you have to watch out for:

- Make sure that you have built up enough trust before asking a turbo question. This is most important if you are persuading, selling or advising.
- Make sure you pace turbo questions so that your conversation partner doesn't get the feeling they are being interrogated.
- Reinforce turbo questions with other active listening skills. Do not give up if you do not receive a complete answer immediately. Help the other person to create new information by listening actively.

In-depth questioning

By asking supplementary questions, you stimulate the other person to be more concrete and you give the impression that you are truly interested. With in-depth questioning, it is important to ask questions which are as neutral as possible in order to avoid coming across as threatening. That is why you should first ask a general and open question and then work towards specific points, according to the lobster pot model. Remember to listen until the other person is finished and ask yourself if the topic has been sufficiently covered before moving on.

Summary

Reiterating what your conversation partner has told you in your own concise words is a difficult but powerful skill. If you summarize information in this way, you will achieve several goals at once:

- You show that you are listening to the other person
- You stimulate the other person to give you more information
- You check if you have understood the message correctly
- You prevent misunderstandings and create opportunities to set them straight
- You structure the stream of information
- You discourage the other person from digressing

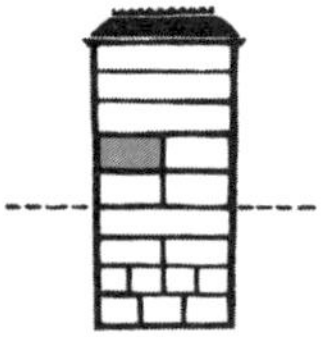

- You give the other person your attention without linking it with a personal opinion
- You acknowledge what the other person is saying

An effective summary has the following characteristics:

- Articulated in your own words
- Objective reflection of the other person's opinion
- Short and to the point
- Reflection of content and feeling
- Formulated as a question

Own words

By using your own words in summarizing what the other person has said, you indicate that you have listened well and understood the information. Make sure that when formulating your summary it does not contain any other, new or incorrect information.

Objective reflection

A good summary reflects your conversation partner's opinion in an undistorted, unbiased manner and does not contain any other ideas than those of the speaker. A summary which is even a little bit subjective often prompts a discussion about the content of the summary. That is why it is so important to keep your opinion in the background and to focus on the other person's opinion, even if you are not in agreement with them.

Short and to the point

A summary has to contain the core of what the other person has said – nothing more, nothing less. Keep it as short as possible: it does not have to be a complete repetition.

Content and feeling

In addition to the factual information contained in the message, a good summary also has to reflect the feeling of the other person. Do not underestimate the value of emotions: often the content is less important than the emotion contained in the story. Listen and watch your conversation partner and do not just register their rational behaviour, but their emotional behaviour as well. In your reflection, give emotion priority above content and try to identify this as clearly as possible. Do not forget to express understanding of the other person's feelings when necessary, because by doing so in the case of irritation, you can moderate the feelings somewhat. By indicating that you understand how the other person feels, they feel that they can trust you.

Formulated as a question
By concluding a summary with a question mark, you indicate that you are open to a response. In this way you create for yourself the possibility of checking if you have understood the information while giving the other person the opportunity to disagree with your summary.

Next steps

Which steps you take after this level depend on the type of conversation you are having. Usually you can now provide your conversation partner with information or convince them about something.

Difficulty with listening?

If you find it difficult to listen to someone attentively, this may be caused by the following:
- Your head is full
- You feel emotion or resistance

A Full Head
It is of course entirely possible that while you are listening to someone you have so much on your mind that it is hard for you to con-

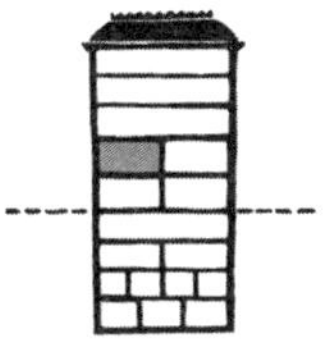

centrate on the conversation. This can make it difficult to put yourself in the other person's shoes or to really absorb what they are saying. Apart from any other unrelated concerns, it may be that it is your own agenda for the conversation that is causing the log jam. Because you want to accomplish something with your conversation partner, it puts pressure on the situation which can lead to you not taking enough time to listen to her. If you want to provide good advice, sell a fantastic product or have thought of a brilliant solution, maybe you can't wait to have your turn to speak, which means you are not leaving enough time and space for listening. If this sounds familiar, it is a good idea to figure out what you need in order to give your full attention to the other person. Adequate self-management, which clears your head for the conversation can prevent a lack of alertness. The realization that your success is dependent on (your attention for) the other person can also motivate you to focus on the other person despite hectic circumstances.

Emotion or resistance

A contentious or stressful relationship with your conversation partner can give you a strong urge to tell your own story and not listen to theirs. It is also possible that the information provided is confrontational or emotional for you, or it scares you. Maybe you have your reservations about what is being said. Whatever the case: the more you become aware of what is bothering you, the better position you will be in to choose your behaviour rather than allowing your emotions to have free rein.

23

Level +1B1: providing information

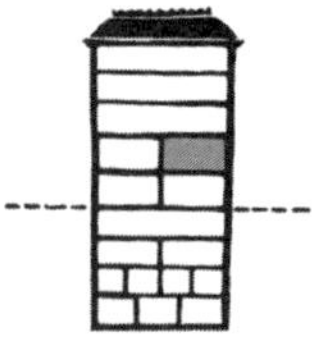

After you have listened and established which information or knowledge your conversation partner needs, you can now give it to him. Any information or knowledge which he doesn't have can be passed on at this level.

Practical tips

If you are going to provide information, it is important to take the following aspects into account:

- Readiness to listen
- Understanding and remembering: structure
- Logical construction of the content
- Keep it interesting: variation, examples and distractions
- Acceptance: harmonizing with the other person, credibility, dealing with reactions

Readiness to listen

The first condition of an effective transfer of information is that your conversation partner must be open to receiving information from you. You can exercise influence over this process by making agreements in the opening of the conversation and giving him enough space to have his say about this. You create this space with your attention and interest. You also create a situation where your conversation partner is prepared to give his attention to what you have to say.

Understanding and remembering: structure

People often overestimate another person's ability to understand and remember what they have been told. That is why it is important at first to limit the amount of information you provide to the essence of the issue. In addition to the amount of information, the manner in which you present it can determine the effect it has on your conversation partner. The more structure you bring to your story by ordering the information well and articulating your logic, the better able your conversation partner will be to understand and remember your story.

A commonly used technique for structuring information is the so-called head-body-tail method. When opening the conversation you establish a framework by explaining what you are about to say, in what sequence you plan to say it and why you are doing so (the head). Following that, you share the body of your story, which you can do to greater effect by presenting your information in points which correspond to the sequence you already indicated. Using a logical construction of the information increases the power of your story. You end with the tail, where you give a short summary of the information and link it to a conclusion. That way you make the information accessible to your conversation partner and ensure that they can absorb the new information easily.

Logical construction of the content

As far as the content of your story goes, the best method is to work from familiar to unfamiliar, concrete to abstract, general to specific and so on. Your conversation partner is then able to start out from familiar ground in your story and subsequently 'travel with you' to terra incognita. This is the best way to connect with your conversation partner and enhances the likelihood that he will really absorb the information.

Keep it interesting: variation, examples and distractions

You can help your conversation partner to remain attentive to your story by varying your voice in tempo, tone and volume. Additionally, you can make the information more vibrant by using fitting and recognizable examples. Using non-verbal communication can also give your story a boost, for example, gestures, eye contact and an active posture. But watch out: non-verbal communication can also detract from your information. If you distract your conversation partner with all sorts of movement (and ticks), if you do not make eye contact or you undermine your credibility in other ways, you weaken the information you are sharing.

Acceptance: harmonizing with the other person, credibility, dealing with reactions

In general, you stimulate people's attention by giving them information which fits into their own frame of reference. If your conversation partner sees their situation or interests reflected in your information, they will more likely be open to it and appreciate it more. That is why it is wise to do your research beforehand, so that you are better able to tailor your story to suit your audience. Direct the information you want to transfer towards the information needs and interests of the other person. Show them what they can do with the information, how they can influence the situation with it or what advantages they can expect from it. Give them the space to respond and ask questions and ask questions of your own. That way, you involve the other person in your story and you check how much information has actually been absorbed.

Examples

A sailing instructor to his students:

'Okay, you can now sail a course, tack and make sightings. We are now going to combine these skills to make a weather shore landing. This type of landing consists of three steps: first check out the landing area, then make a sighting and finally land going into the wind. Let's go through these steps in detail.

Step 1: Before you make a landing, it is essential that you locate a good place to do so. A suitable landing place depends on what you plan to do. Are you going to stay a few seconds or a few days? Sail past the landing place a few times and look for any obstacles above and under the water. What is the wind doing and is it still a weather shore? How easily can you sail off again if the manoeuvre fails?

Step 2: For a controlled landing, it is important that during the manoeuvre you sail a course into the wind. To establish your course, sail into the wind on the tack opposite to that which you will land on. Now check the place where you want to land. If it is at a 90 degree angle to you, then you can tack and you will be on the right line into the wind to reach your landing place.

Step 3: Once you are on the right course, luff your jib so that it's not catching any wind. By pulling the mainsheet in and letting it out, you can control the speed of the boat. Make sure you don't lose speed too quickly. You won't be able to point as well and you will lose your course into the wind.

Summary: First think ahead and choose a landing place wisely. Then make a sighting to choose the correct line into the wind. Finally, control your speed with the mainsheet and gently approach your chosen landing site. Are there any questions?'

A trainer to his group:

'We are going to brainstorm. It is important to start by formulating the right question. When brainstorming, the following rules apply:

- Everything that is said is good
- Everything that is said is written down
- You can always elaborate on other people's ideas
- No criticism of ideas expressed is allowed (this is a critical condition)
- We can try a practice round first if you want

Write the question you want to brainstorm about on the flip chart and note down all the responses. Encourage each other to come up with as many ideas as possible. If there are any criticisms, they must be saved for the discussion after the brainstorming session.

Summary: A good question, rules and a practice round if needed. During the brainstorming the flow of ideas must be kept going, ideas may not be criticized and you record the results on the flip chart.'

Difficulty providing information?

If you are presenting information, it is important that you really know your subject. If that is not the case, it will be difficult to explain it with confidence and in a structured manner. Not only the content, but also the situation in which you are presenting the information can lead to insecurity. If you are speaking to a powerful delegation or a large group, the tension can prevent you from giving your best performance. In situations such as this, a certain level of stress is normal, even useful, but sometimes it can be so crushing that is has a crippling effect on you. If you often feel like this, it may be interesting to examine where your insecurity comes from. The more aware you are of the source of the problem, the better able you will be to let it go.

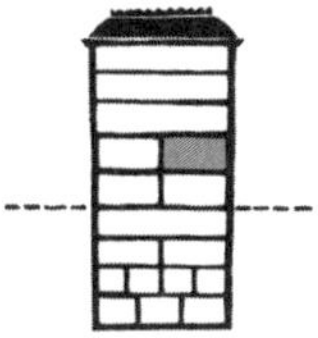

24

Providing information in special situations

There are three situations where you have information that the other does not have, but needs. This gives rise to the need for a conversation initiated solely by you. Obviously, that the information is introduced early on in the conversation. In these situations, you begin by sharing the information rather than listening first. The three situations are the following:

- Discussing specific challenges
- Giving feedback
- Communicating bad news

Discussing specific challenges

This type of challenge is nothing more than an irritation or a problem you are having that you want to discuss with the other person. Or preferably: that has to be discussed to prevent (further) endangering the relationship. The motivation for discussing the issue probably existed before the conversation actually began. Prior to the conversation, something happened which you would like to talk to your conversation partner about. Examples include situations in which the other person did not follow through on agreements or in which you feel short-changed by the other person for one reason or another. You begin this type of conversation by indicating that you have something to discuss.

Practical tips

If you bring up difficulties of this sort, the art is to formulate your message clearly and plainly, without provoking a lot of emotion or resistance in your conversation partner. Most of the time emotion plays a role with you as well. That is why it is important during your preparation for this type of conversation to gauge how emotional you yourself feel in the situation and where those emotions come from. A lot of the time, your emotions are not related to your conversation partner or the situation, but come from a previous experience which is totally unrelated to the situation and the person in question. Some of your emotions are part of the situation, but – in many cases – they are not. If you bring too much (extra) emotion into the conversation and blame your conversation partner a disproportionate amount, they will feel that you are being unfair. There is a big chance that they will go on the defensive and the conversation can easily turn into an argument.

To prevent this and still make it possible to discuss the issue in question, I advise you to explain what you mean as simply as possible. You can do this by examining exactly what type of behaviour your conversation partner exhibited, what they did or did not do and what they could have done differently, according to you. The more exactly you can describe the behaviour, the clearer it will be to the other person. The more factually you approach the situation, the less likely they will be offended by it. Furthermore, the chance is greater that the message will come across clearly. You can increase this clarity even more by pointing out the consequences of your conversation partner's behaviour rather than merely mentioning the behaviour itself. In some cases, the consequences are concrete and demonstrable: the reckless driving that led to a dent in the car or the long telephone call that resulted in a sky-high bill are clear and demonstrable results. But in practice, the consequences of undesirable behaviour are not always so concrete. Consequences can also involve a certain risk, such as endangering your relationship with one of your clients. Consequences can also be found in your feelings: worry, disappointment or sadness on your part are certainly consequences that another person should take into account.

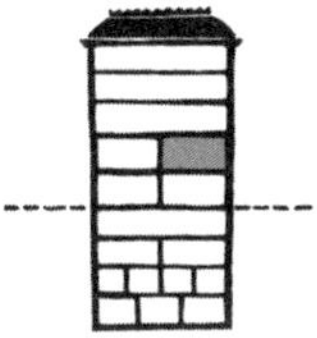

When discussing this type of issue your tone and posture are important. If you come across as too intense, you run the risk of your conversation partner clamming up and things ending in an impasse. Recognize that very few people take criticism well. Keep your tone and body language as friendly and constructive as possible, without detracting from the seriousness of what you want to discuss. Many times, your conversation partner will already suspect that you are not too pleased about something they have done or neglected to do.

Examples

Discussing an issue with a chatty senior colleague:
'I notice that you keep interrupting me when we are negotiating with our contacts. In our conversation this morning you did not let me finish what I was saying at least three times. I am having trouble dealing with this and I'm afraid our clients will take us less seriously because of it. How do you see this issue?'

Discussing your concern with an incautious radiologist:
'I've noticed lately that you are getting more and more careless when using your lead apron. Today you were not wearing your apron correctly or at all during two examinations. Not only is this dangerous for your own health, it is also setting a bad example for the interns and junior staff in the department. What do you think?'

Next steps

Once you have cleared up the problem, give your conversation partner the opportunity to respond. In the best case scenario, you will get a tumble of words defending or mitigating the circumstances under which the behaviour was exhibited. Often, your conversation partner will be a little startled by the fact that they have been challenged about this behaviour. Listen sympathetically, and let them know that you are not out to make them feel small and allow them the room to find some acknowledgement coming from you. Do not get defensive and respond with a counter attack, let them finish speaking and listen closely. Listening is often enough to allow your point to sink in so that your conversation partner comes up with their own ideas for improving things in future.

Even if the other person brings up reasons why they are unable to change their behaviour, listening is still, in the first place, the best advice. After some time has gone by, people with these types of reactions usually come around, after which you can look for a good solution together. The same goes for situations where your conversation partner trades tit for tat and makes a comment about your behaviour. Ask what's bothering him. If you are prepared to deal with his remarks seriously, there is a greater chance that he will react positively to your observation.

Naturally, there is the risk that the conversation could derail as a result of your discussion of the issue. Depending on your conversation partner's reaction, choose the condition forming level which will help you deal with this reaction, for example, the emotion or hidden opposition and influence level. The latter is applicable if your conversation partner remains defensive or tries another tactic to avoid what you want to talk about.

Difficulty discussing specific challenges?

If you notice that you find it difficult to discuss certain issues, you can examine what lies at the root of your trouble. Check to see if one of the following insights might be applicable to your experiences...

Difficulty with confrontation

If you find it difficult to discuss problems in general, then it might be because you do not like to confront or hurt people. That may be an integral part of your personality, but for many people this difficulty stems from practical considerations. The person who is critical of others, opens themselves up for attack. It is often easier – and in a group often more diplomatic – to keep issues to yourself and leave it up to others to bring them up. But recognize that by doing so you are endangering your relationship with the person in question and may (later) hurt them more than is necessary. Once the bomb eventually bursts, it will be charged with extra emotion and a confusing and risky situation will arise.

Is it even worthwhile with this conversation partner?

If you find it difficult to bring up your problem in a certain situation, then it might be due to your estimation of the situation and the reaction you expect from your conversation partner. It is possible that you think it is of no use because the other person can or will not change. Maybe you are afraid that you will not to be taken seriously. I advise you to reserve these types of conclusions until you have made a serious attempt to discuss the issue. If you do not do this, you are thinking for the other person and you are not giving them a chance to respond to what you have to say to them. And you run the risk of unfairly labelling him as unapproachable.

Negative reactions when discussing specific challenges

If you often get negative reactions when discussing certain issues, it is important to examine what aspects of your behaviour rub people the wrong way. Maybe your points sound too much like blame or criticism, or someone feels your approach is a personal condemnation rather than a problem with specific behaviour. A calm, factual and respectful tactic seldom leads to unpleasant reactions.

Giving feedback

The term feedback comes from system analysis and is applied to several branches of science (including physics, biology and psychology).

Feedback is a form of system control where data about the output is fed back into the system to exert influence on the input. In fact, feedback is a reaction, verbal or non-verbal, to a preceding action, verbal or non-verbal (Engel et al., 1986). *Feedback loops*, as they are shown schematically in figure 1 can be observed everywhere. For example, in the way in which you drive a car: with small corrections in steering you keep the car on the road. When you run off course, you register the fact and connect it with the need to correct your steering (feedback), after which you take the necessary action.

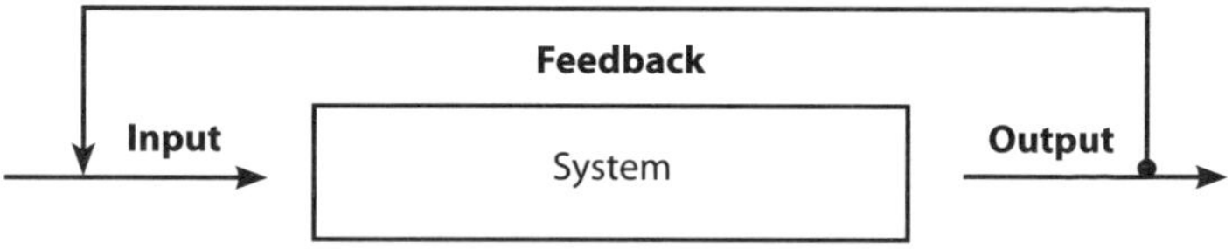

Figure 1 Feedback loop

There are two types of feedback: positive and negative. With negative feedback, deviations from a standard are corrected, which minimizes them and creates a stable situation. With positive feedback, deviations, fluctuations, shifts and changes are reinforced, which makes the sys-

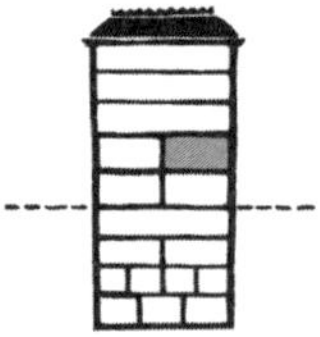

tem less stable. Negative feedback leads to stability, positive feedback to change. Steering a car is an example of a negative feedback loop, as are temperature adjustments via a thermostat. A swing which continually gets a push is an example of a positive feedback loop.

It is important to remember that negative feedback leads to stability and control: the system is cleansed of changes and motion.

On the other hand, positive feedback reinforces change by adding energy, which creates more intense movement. In contact between people, feedback works in a comparable way. Corrective, negative feedback helps you to determine which behaviour you need to change to improve your performance but threatens energy, motivation and ability to change. Motivating, positive feedback is a powerful encouragement to build on effective behaviour.

Giving feedback (in the narrow definition of this book) is commenting on behavioural observations in order to support another person's learning process. That means we are only dealing with the learning process of the person who is receiving the feedback. So the person who is giving feedback should consider the interests of the receiver and not (as mentioned in discussing challenges and setting limits) their own interests. This distinction is important in determining the degree to which the receiver is prepared to hear the feedback and do something with the information.

A feedback situation arises if you have had the opportunity to observe the other person's behaviour and discuss it together. A condition for the effectiveness of the feedback is that both people agree to the fact that you are giving feedback.

Feedback is an essential part of working with other people, whether you are a manager or not. You give feedback to your colleagues with the aim of improving their performance. You can do so in a corrective manner, where you indicate how things can be improved, but you can also do so in an edifying manner, where you point out the effective behaviour which already exists.

You can give feedback in various situations: during instructional or training sessions after an exercise, in the workplace or during a conversation. In this chapter, we are assuming a conversation with one person (a staff member or colleague) as a result of your observation of their behaviour.

Practical tips

A feedback conversation begins with an opening in which you introduce the goal of the conversation. Next, move on to the listening and receiving information level by asking the other person how they view their own performance. This is an important step because you give your conversation partner the chance – if necessary – to let off steam and you get an idea of their point of view. If it is clear how they see things, then you can present your feedback. The effectiveness of this is dependent on various factors which will be briefly discussed below.

Feedback has to be clear

Only when you clearly indicate what is good and what can be better do you give the other person the opportunity to do something with your feedback. This means that you have to clearly word your observations of the other person's behaviour and, if possible, supplement this with examples. When you give feedback which is too generally worded, there is a chance that the other person will not have a good enough starting point to change their behaviour.

Give feedback as soon as possible

Your feedback has the greatest effect if you give it as soon as possible after observing specific behaviour. If you wait (too) long before giving feedback, there is less chance that you can explain the behaviour and its effects clearly. Furthermore, it is not impossible that the other person no longer remembers what you are talking about.

Base feedback on performance profile

By basing your feedback on the performance profile of the person it is meant for, you increase the chance that the feedback will fall on fertile ground and that the other person will actually do something with it. That is why it is wise to determine the other person's performance profile before undertaking the conversation. Are you dealing with a *high achiever* or a *low achiever*?

High achievers are people who love to learn, have a great deal of self-confidence and are personally motivated to perform to the best of their ability. Low achievers are usually insecure about their performance, looking for affirmation and exhibit resistance to changing their behaviour or are even scared to. In determining your evaluation, it is important to remember that a performance profile is situational (dependent on the subject or theme): someone can be a high achiever in one area and a low achiever in another.

High achievers:

- Often ask lots of questions
- Have an active posture
- Want to experiment a lot
- Have a critical attitude
- Experience change as a challenge

Low achievers:

- Have a negative attitude towards change
- Make a lot of 'Yes, but...' remarks during conversations about performance
- Are insecure when they are trying out new skills
- Ask few questions
- Are not open to new information

High achievers are hungry for feedback. They want to know exactly what they can improve on and for this reason get the most from negative feedback. That is why you should be as specific as possible in suggesting improvements, but do not omit (specific) positive feedback as well. Low achievers like to receive affirmation for what they do and therefore respond better to positive feedback. They are not (yet) open to suggestions for improvement. Negative feedback tends to make low achievers only more insecure. In order to give effective feedback, it is best if you focus on effective behaviour, as trivial as it may be. By doing so, you increase both the receiver's self-confidence and their motivation.

Dispense feedback in doses

Feedback works best if you limit it to just a few points, and preferably just one. A long summary of good behaviour and behaviour which needs to be improved can be overwhelming for the other person, which makes the feedback unclear and prompts the other person to close off. By focusing on a limited area, you increase the chance that the other person will actually do something with the feedback you give and improve their behaviour.

Distinguish validating (positive) and corrective (negative) feedback

A clear distinction between both forms of feedback prevents one form being overshadowed by the other which can have the effect of being unclear. Try to cluster feedback about effective and less effective behaviour.

Tips to prevent resistance to feedback

To increase the level of acceptance of your feedback and to avoid resistance, you should take the following into consideration:

- Play the ball, not the player
- Give feedback in terms of behaviour and its effects, rather than only your judgment (good or bad)
- Do not give feedback to someone who is emotional or irritated

Examples

Validating (positive) feedback from sales manager to sales person: 'You gave the client a chance to articulate her resistance first before responding. That made the client calm and prepared to hear your side of the story.'

Corrective (negative) feedback from sales manager to sales person: 'You gave the client a big concession way too early in the game without asking for anything in return. That gave her the idea that your initial offer was unreasonable and that there were more concessions for her snap up if she had just exerted more pressure.'

Giving feedback for experts: shaping

When evaluating others' behaviour, usually the things which are not going well stand out the most. This increases the risk that you automatically end up in a corrective (negative) feedback loop, which can have a blocking, de-motivating effect on the other person. The enormous power of validating (positive) feedback therefore often remains unused in practice. If positive feedback is given at all, this often remains limited to a general, obligatory remark which is made as a lead-up to what is about to come (read: a correction).

It can be different. Well worded and presented specific positive feedback has been demonstrated to be the most effective way to influence behaviour (Skinner, 1966). To give feedback in this manner, known as *shaping* in psychology, you need insight about the material you are giving feedback about. To clarify this, I will give you an example of a situation in which a staff member receives feedback about the way in which they handle complaints. The behavioural aspects which play a role are self-control, understanding, listening comprehension, posing questions, presenting solutions and making agreements.

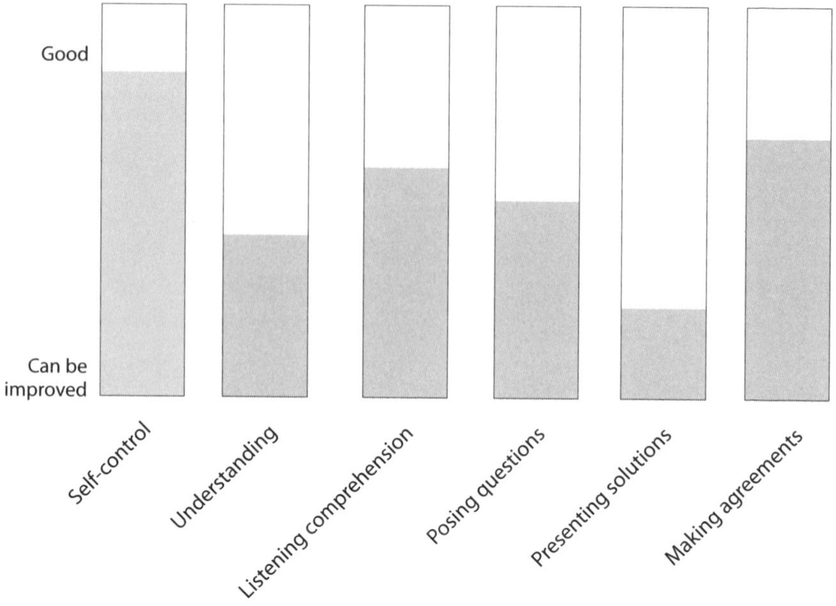

Figure 2 Behaviour elements for dealing effectively with complaints; mastery level of the intern from the example

Partner of a law firm to an intern:
'I see a huge improvement. You are good at listening comprehension, at making agreements and following through with them, you ask the right questions and you have iron-willed self-control. This enables you to deal with emotional clients. Keep up the good work!'

By using shaping, you get more out of the people you are giving feedback to. But in order to do that well, you need a great deal of insight into what constitutes the skills to be learned.

Before you give someone feedback, you have to observe them in practice, which enables you to see if and to what extent they possesses the specific important competencies. During this observation you do not focus so much on the shortcomings you see, but specifically on the things which are going well.

Next steps

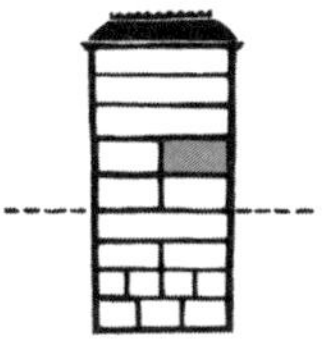

After you have given your feedback, it is a good idea to allow the receiver to respond. In doing so, listen calmly and do not be quick to argue, even if you get a 'Yes, but...' reaction. Keep asking questions and see how your conversation partner takes the feedback. Ultimately, they decide what they will do with your feedback. Maybe afterwards you can both consider ways in which the other person can reduce their less effective behaviour.

Difficulty with giving feedback?

Problems in giving feedback can arise because you yourself do not have a good idea of the relevant competencies or the development path of the person to whom you are giving feedback. This can make the feedback vague and it will be difficult for the other person to learn from it. Also, if you want to communicate too much feedback at once, it can be difficult to take it all in. That is why for effective feedback: 'less is more.' Establish your priorities beforehand when addressing development points so that you can aim appropriately and hit your target with only a few shots.

Another problem in giving feedback is the degree of acceptance of your feedback or you as the person giving it. You do not receive acceptance if you just start giving feedback without making agreements beforehand, or if you present your evaluation as the only truth. Giving feedback in this manner comes very close to giving criticism. Feedback is distinguished from criticism by giving the other person explicit acknowledgement of their freedom to determine their behaviour themselves. Feedback must be able to be viewed as an opinion, which the other person may or may not choose to do something with. You indicate how the other person's behaviour comes across, without linking this with a concrete request to change this behaviour. The other person then has the choice as to how and if they will change their behaviour. This is contrary to criticism, where there is a demand to change.

Communicating bad news

Bad news is negative information arising from actual situations or irrevocable decisions. The message can per definition not be negotiated and that means that delivering it requires a specific approach. Bad news can include a death notification or a dismissal, but it can also include a 'no', an extended delivery time or explaining that agreements cannot be fulfilled.

In short, there are two types of conversations involving bad news. The first type consists of information that you had beforehand and which you suspect will be bad news for the other person. The bad news in this case is the concrete reason for the conversation.

The second type arises during the conversation, for example, if your conversation partner asks you for something which you can or will not give or if the bad news you mentioned earlier does not seem to have sunk in. In these situations it becomes necessary over the course of the conversation – more or less unexpectedly – to share bad news.

Practical tips

With both types, it is best to give the bad news as quickly as possible. This is not only in your interest, but also in the interest of your conversation partner. After all, the bad news often forms the framework within which the conversation will be continued and furthermore any other subjects to be discussed will be coloured by it once it is out in the open. As long as the message is not out in the open, there is a big chance that the rest of the conversation will be irrelevant and you may lose your conversation partner's attention for what is relevant. Even worse: if you keep the bad news to yourself, later on the other person can feel that they have has been misled. The fact that you did not inform them can be experienced as an imbalance of power and they can associate this with a feeling of inferiority. Remaining silent about bad news can moreover lead to the other person being unclear about your

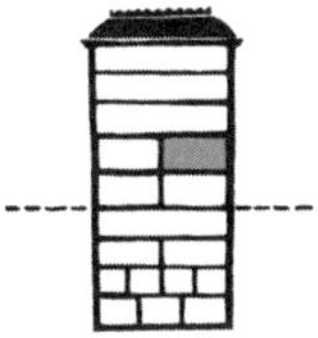

limits, they can continually pressure you to move in a direction you do not want to – or cannot — go (Vrolijk, 1997).

It is not easy to communicate bad news well – which is why people often try to soften the blow or postpone the moment when they have to deliver it. These are avoidance strategies which stem from a desire to avoid the recipient, and which only result in the effects of the bad news being negatively reinforced. This leads to more frustration and more intense emotions – to an unnecessary mess that you will have to clean up afterwards. Furthermore, as the bearer of bad news, using these types of strategies you run the risk of the recipient's negative emotions being directed at you.

Avoidance strategies which you should not use when communicating bad news include:

- Sugar coating the pill
- 'Hang yourself'
- 'Tell and run'

Sugar coating the pill

By only emphasizing the positive side of the bad news you are sending the message that the other person should be happy about the bad news. But if you are really dealing with bad news, the other person will have no desire to see the positive side; it only causes the situation to become more confusing and complex.

'Hang yourself'

Making allusions and dropping hints in hopes that the other person will guess at the bad news may seem like an easy way out for you as the messenger, but the effect of this is that your conversation partner often feels deceived. This strategy usually leads to an even more complicated situation.

'Tell and run'

Communicating the bad news quickly and then ending the conversation immediately afterwards is clearly evasive behaviour. A variant of this is sending the news in written form, via email or even text messaging or having someone else announce it. For the fearful among us, this may seem attractive, but this method of communication only increases the negative effect of the message. The messenger cannot see the recipient's reaction and affect it since it is taking place outside their view and sphere of influence. If you use this strategy, emotional obligations remain between you and the recipient which can lead to a very uncomfortable situation in any future meetings.

What is a good strategy then? The best way to give bad news is to formulate it clearly and concisely and tell it like it is. Do not belittle it, but do not blow it out of proportion either. Say it immediately and do not beat around the bush. Then you have said your piece and you can focus on the other person. Moreover, you are not keeping them on tenterhooks and they know what they are facing. Apart from that, you should not lose sight of good manners: a short and sympathetic introduction is certainly not out of place. But do not make one before you deliver the news, otherwise you may never get around to doing so or you may fall into sugar coating the pill.

Not only is giving an elaborate prelude to the bad news risky, but – for whatever reason – so is speaking about it for too long after delivering it. After you have made the announcement, it is a good idea to allow your conversation partner a chance to respond – after all, they have just received bad news that they may like to say something about. Give the other person the time to process the news. Do not begin an explanation, but wait for a reaction. And if it isn't forthcoming, ask for it. If it seems that the bad news has not sunk in, repeat it calmly and clearly.

Examples

A project that has been cancelled:
'Hannah, sit down for a moment. Unfortunately I have to inform you that we will not be going ahead with your project as of 1 January. Lately it seems that you assumed that the project would go ahead one way or another, but I want to be clear about this: after 1 January it is definitely over.'

'No is no':
'Mr. Johnson. In response to your request for credit: our bank has examined your situation extensively based on the details you provided and we have come to the conclusion that we unfortunately cannot grant you a loan.'

Next steps

You can assume that everyone who hears bad news, to a greater or lesser degree, will be dealing with emotions. Before you can move on to other things, feelings will have to calm down. You can stimulate this by giving your conversation partner the opportunity to express their emotions, and possibly by identifying the emotions that you see them experiencing. In this type of situation you will have to go back to the emotional level where feelings can be expressed and discharged.

The way in which people respond to bad news varies widely. The reaction depends on the trust between you and the recipient, their personality and the degree to which the bad news affects them, among other things. Another factor is the question as to whether or not the bad news was expected. Below follow a few examples of typical reactions to bad news.

Asking questions

It is common for people who are confronted with bad news first to ask the messenger a lot of questions. This is a tricky response because if the recipient is very emotional your answers may lead to more emotions. That is why you should keep in mind that if your conversation partner responds with questions your next step will be on the emotion conversation level. Try to gauge whether or not they really want an answer or if the questions are just a run-up to an emotional outburst. If you suspect that the other person is asking questions as a prelude to an intense reaction, keep your answers short and relatively superficial. In such a situation your answers will most likely be used as a weapon and you may waste important arguments which your conversation partner will find acceptable at a later stage. As an alternative you can answer the question by repeating the bad news or by summarizing feelings. To illustrate this, two responses are outlined below (as a continuation of the examples in the previous paragraph):

The cancelled project:

'How so? Why must my project be scrapped while other projects get the green light?'

'I can see that you are having trouble swallowing this.'

'Yes, it's ridiculous. The project is just about to bear fruit. It is probably a political decision to do this...'

'No is no':

'Why not then? It was a reasonable request wasn't it? I figured out all the details and made calculations, what is the problem?'

'You do not understand why we have made this decision?'

'No, I am one hundred percent sure of my business and I think it's pathetic that the bank cannot see its way to aiding me in my enterprise...'

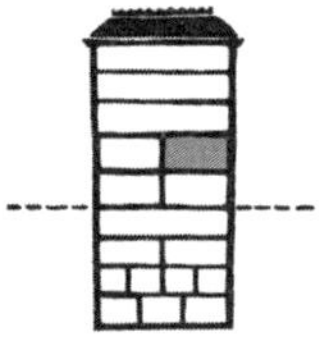

Anger

If the recipient expresses frustration through irritation and rage, it can be difficult to handle. Try and remember that the rage is not aimed at you, but is a reaction to the bad news. The emotion conversation level can give you tips on how to deal with this. To sound out whether the emotions have subsided enough to continue the conversation without problems, you carefully prick your conversation partner's balloon as it were by asking questions and seeing how they respond. If no more air comes out of the balloon, then their feelings have calmed down.

Sadness

Sadness can be expressed through crying, but also through silence and sometimes the urge to walk away. Try and keep the other person involved in the conversation and point out what you see if they do not say anything. Deal with the emotion at the appropriate conversation level.

Negotiation

If the recipient tries to turn the bad news into a point for negotiation in looking for wiggle room, then it is of little use to give that room. Your message is after all non-negotiable. In that case, repeat the bad news and focus attention on the emotions involved if necessary.

Denial

Some people do not want to face the confrontation of the message and deny it steadfastly. The news sometimes has to be repeated more than once before they are prepared to let it sink in. In that case, repeat the message calmly and check carefully to see if the news has penetrated.

If you have to communicate bad news to someone who is directly or indirectly responsible, it can be rather vexing. Even more vexing is if, in your view, the recipient had no influence on the bad news.

The most vexing of all is if you or the organization you work for did something which is bad news for the other person. This situation does not require a different approach, except that you have to stand even firmer and be on the lookout for pitfalls because the temptation to fall into them is greater. Do not try and soften the news and avoid getting all too caught up in the emotions of the recipient!

Moving on after the first response

In the 'ideal' situation, you will get an emotional reaction to bad news. Once steam has been released and you notice that the other person can think straight again, you can provide them with an explanation based on the giving information conversation level. In bad news conversations, you usually go into arguments or reasons which led up to the bad news. To prevent the other person getting into a dispute with you, it is a good idea to use only the best arguments. Do not bring up too many reasons, but just the strongest points and present these one by one. Keep in mind that each argument may result in the emotion rearing up and respond to this by shifting back to the emotion conversation level. You can end by making agreements within the framework of the bad news on the problem solving level.

Bad news is unalterable, but often you can reduce its consequences by both looking for ways to minimize the negative effects for your conversation partner and keep them within limits. You can do this on the value adding negotiations/problem solving conversation level, which you will read more about in chapter 29. Let the other person help think of possible solutions. Although they have no influence on the bad news, they can take responsibility for solving their own problems.

Keep in mind that solutions within the framework of bad news are not accepted quickly if the bad news itself has not yet been accepted. You have to pay close attention to timing in this case. If you present possible solutions too early, the other person will view these as attempts to 'make it up.' In order to determine if the emotions have

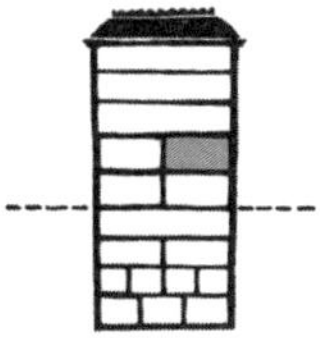

really subsided and the way is clear to make agreements, you can ask the other person the following question: 'What would you like, given the situation?' If you get an emotional reaction, then there is still work to be done on the emotion level. If you get a meaningful response, then you can move on to the value adding negotiations/problem solving level.

Difficulty with communicating bad news?

If you are capable of communicating bad news without inhibitions, then you are one of the few. Most people find it hard to disappoint others and deal with their intense emotions. Additionally, people worry about working together in the future. Do not allow these feelings to keep you from giving bad news in a straightforward manner without delay because that really is the best way for all concerned parties to deal with difficult circumstances!

25

Level +1B2: persuasion and advice

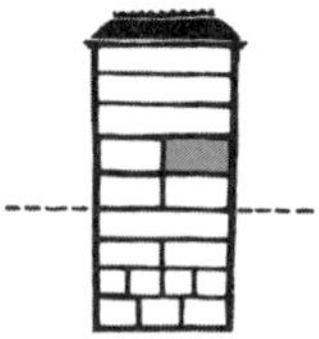

If you would like to influence someone without exercising formal or hierarchal power, then you end up in a situation involving persuasion. If you simply do not have any power over the other person, then persuasion is your only option. And if you do have the power, you do not always want to use it since this can cause negative reactions. The ability to persuade others is therefore very useful to everyone, whether they enjoy a position of power or not.

Persuasion is essentially different from pressuring or manipulating your conversation partner. It is also quite different to the political game of building up enough influence via coalitions and the power of others to force your conversation partner to concur with your ideas.

Persuasion, according to the winning dialogue system, begins with understanding the interests of your conversation partner. Next, you think of the most appropriate suggestion which you formulate in such a way that your conversation partner chooses to go along with it. The acknowledgement of your conversation partner's freedom of choice to agree to your proposal or not is a condition of the winning dialogue persuasion situation. If you attempt to limit your conversation partner's freedom of choice, then you are not using persuasion, but rather tactics such as force and (emotional) manipulation. You are placing your own interests above those of the other person – which is in conflict with the basic principles of this book – and creating a situation in which your conversation partner will feel uncomfortable to some degree.

Many salespeople who are otherwise enthusiastic and motivated and have a good business sense miss the boat on this point. In their frenzy to score, they often unconsciously employ techniques which limit the freedom of choice of potential buyers – often with an adverse effect. If you truly concentrate on the interests of your conversation partner and deal with this knowledge in such a way that they can choose to accept your proposal or not, you have a greater chance of achieving positive results and establishing a long term relationship.

A situation involving persuasion actually begins on the introducing structure level. Subsequently you listen to the other person to get an idea of their situation and needs so that you can establish a framework for yourself which you can use to present your proposition.

Practical tips

Many of the instructions for providing information (level +1B1) also apply to this conversation level. You conversation partner's situation is the framework into which your proposal must fit. This framework is formed by the external conditions which your proposal must fulfil in order to be accepted, as well as by the needs of the other person.

Needs

Your conversation partner's needs can actually be seen as a gap between their current and ideal situation. They form the motivation for the other person to change something. If you want to persuade them, not only will you have to know what their needs are, but you will also have to make a proposition which fits those needs as well as possible. The more aware you are of their needs, the greater the chance that you will succeed in getting your proposal accepted.

Features

Your proposal must show how you can close the gap between your conversation partner's current and ideal situations within the applicable external conditions. The external conditions are determined on one hand by what you can offer and on the other hand by the degree to which your options fit in with the other person's situation. Therefore, you choose the advice, idea or product that best matches up with their needs. This establishes the features of your proposal and you can now only choose which features you wish to explain when you go to discuss your proposition. It is of course up to you to focus more attention on specific, relevant features than on less relevant features. An example:

Say a client at a Volkswagen dealer wants a hatchback which can fit two adults and two children. The car cannot cost more than 25,000 euro. After the salesperson has gathered enough information about the client by asking specific questions, he can advise a Golf or a Polo. After a few more questions, the salesperson can narrow his suggestion to the Golf with a few extras. This establishes the features of his proposal. In order to stimulate the sale, he explains a few of the features which are relevant and interesting to the client. Because the salesperson has discovered that her safety and that of her family is of the utmost importance to the client, the salesperson decides it is a good idea to talk about the inflatable curtains and link these with the client's need for safety.

If the salesperson mentioned the inflatable curtains without any further explanation or linking relevant benefits to the client, the client may not (sufficiently) see the advantages of such; she simply would not recognize them. It is not always possible for a client to see what a proposal contains and how it relates to his or her needs without an explanation. Even if the salesperson praises the option by associating it with irrelevant benefits, for example, by pointing out that the car is much easier to resell because of that feature, the client would not see this as an interesting option.

If the salesperson mentions a feature irrelevant to the client, for example that the car comes standard equipped with air conditioning, it will have little or no effect on the client's intention to buy. Furthermore: the salesperson would only provoke more resistance to the tune of: 'I don't need those extra luxuries, but I will probably have to pay for them', and: 'I never use that anyway, it only uses more fuel.'

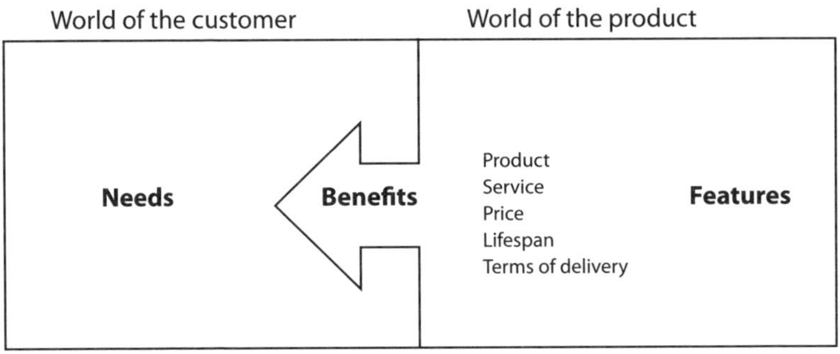

Figure 1 Linking features to needs via benefits

Benefits link the connection between the (unchangeable) features of your proposition (your advice, product or idea) and the equally unchangeable needs of your conversation partner. Benefits are, as it were, the glue that holds together the relevant features of your proposal and the needs of your conversation partner.

Examples of features:

- A feature of an electronic agenda is the alarm function.
- A feature of a bungalow is that all of the rooms are on one level.

You can link various benefits to each feature of your proposal. The art is to select and formulate these benefits so that they best match the situations and needs of the other person. Since one feature can equal a different benefit to different people, in principle there are no generally applicable benefits. The value of a benefit is determined by the individual circumstances. One benefit of a mobile phone is that you are available everywhere and at all times. For people who prefer peace and quiet, this advantage is actually a disadvantage.

You therefore have to decide which benefits will advance your proposal in the eyes of the person you are trying to persuade. In doing so, you match up the benefits of the proposal with their needs. Only positive and relevant benefits can effectively persuade another person; irrelevant benefits threaten the success of your conversation because they cloud the relevant benefits – and therefore detract from their effect.

Feature: This car has a 3.2-litre engine.
Benefit 1: This car accelerates quickly.
Benefit 2: This car is very quiet.
Benefit 3: This car has a high maximum speed.
Benefit 4: In this car you do not have to shift gear often.

Benefits 1 and 3 would be attractive to someone who is interested in status and sporty driving, while benefits 2 and 4 might be useful to a client who values comfortable and peaceful driving.

The feature of a well organized trip is that everything is agreed on and arranged ahead of time.
Benefit 1: The probability of nasty surprises is small.
Benefit 2: The costs are known in advance.
Benefit 3: Everything on the list can be visited.
Benefit 4: You do not have to arrange much else, so you can relax completely.

It is also true in this example that different benefits are relevant to different people.

To persuade the other person it is obvious that you have to present your proposal with enthusiasm. This method shows that you in fact believe in your proposal. That is not unimportant, because if you do not believe in it yourself, why should another person do so? But be aware of the fact that despite your enthusiasm you have to give

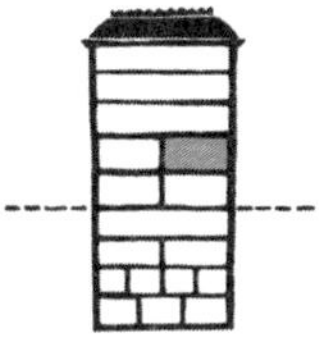

the other person room to form their own opinions!

As indicated above, you can choose which arguments you want to explain in detail. Sometime there are disadvantages associated with your proposal. In that case it is wise to include these in your pitch. Do not sweep them under the rug, but paint a big picture including the gritty details. If you choose to remain silent about the disadvantages, you run the risk that the other person will feel cheated afterwards – and from a long term perspective, that is never good for business.

Examples

You have been hired as an organization advisor by a member of the holding management to resolve problems within an operating company. The director of the operating company is confronted with a vote of no confidence from his management team. You have carried out a quick scan of the organization which shows that the vote of no confidence is just the tip of the iceberg. You report to your client with the goal of carrying out more research before jumping to conclusions and undertaking radical measures. You advice is as follows: 'The most obvious action to take would be to dismiss the general manager or the entire management team and to move forward with (a) replacement(s). But there are indications that there is more going on here: an ambiguous administration of the organization with plenty of differing and indistinct lines. Additionally, there are political games being played within the organization. That is why I suggest that we only take the measures necessary to enable operations to continue for the short term and then perform a more in-depth examination to find out what led to this situation developing. This will enable you to take much more specific measures which will solve the problem more satisfactorily and above all will cause much less collateral damage.'

Next steps

After you have presented your proposal, your conversation partner will (usually) respond. Remain open to that response. Listen closely, especially to any negative comments, and take the time to answer questions. Give the other person the chance to get used to the (new) proposal and do not try and persuade them too quickly or with too much enthusiasm. If they have any objections, you can shift back to the resistance level to clear up any remaining questions and objections which stand in the way of your proposal being accepted. There is a good chance that you can restore the contact and that you can continue on where you left off. Make sure that you do not get into an argument with the other person in dealing with objections or resistance. Recognize that you can easily prevent resistance and objections as long as you know how to give your conversation partner the right information at the right time.

If they do not give any response at all, it is a good idea to ask for one. It is after all important that you know what they think of your proposition. Keep in contact and remain open to the response; if necessary, actively encourage a response. The more interactive your proposal is the better!

In situations where it takes a lot of effort to persuade someone, you will have to put in a lot of work in dealing with resistance. In this case it is useful to gather new information from your conversation partner. You can consider moving temporarily to the listening/receiving information level and then go back to your original conversation level where you can breathe new life into your proposal based on the fresh information that you have.

If your proposal has been accepted, then the best thing to do is move on to the wrapping up and closing deals level in order to reach an agreement about the execution of your proposal. You will usually have to discuss the details more fully. You can best do this in the form of a value adding negotiation (see chapter 29) or, if that doesn't work, with a value sharing negotiation (see chapter 30).

Difficulty with persuasion and advice?

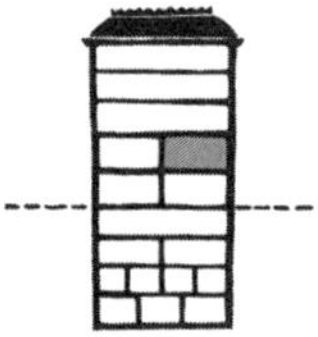

If you often have difficulty with this conversation level, the following insights might help you.

Too many arguments

The phasing of your arguments is critical in a situation involving persuasion. If you mention too many arguments at once, it can arouse suspicion and you also run the risk that your weaker arguments detract from your stronger ones. That is why it is important to mention only the strongest arguments – those which best match up with the needs and situation of the other person. Control yourself, make sure that you are not reasoning too much from your own point of view and do not allow your personal interests to gain the upper hand!

Too much advice or too quickly

Resistance can indicate that you have (temporarily) lost the other person. This can happen because you supplied too much information or because you launched your proposal too quickly. If you do not focus any attention on the resistance, the likelihood of the acceptance of your information will decrease and you may damage your conversation partner's trust, with the possible result being that they throw in the towel or even start working against you. Try to find out what is going on by shifting back to the hidden opposition and influence level so that you can restore your connection.

No personal conviction

If you are not personally convinced of the merits of your proposal it can be very hard to present it to another person in a convincing way. Is it an option to adjust your proposal so that you do stand by it? If that is not possible, then you will have to answer an ethical question: do you really want to convince another person when yourself do not stand by what you are saying?

Too much personal investment

If your own interests play too great a role in your efforts to persuade your conversation partner, you will quickly run into resistance. Nobody likes being pressured. Make sure that in persuasion situations you connect with the other person and stay in touch with your feelings and your intuition in order to pick up on signals of resistance and adjust your behaviour accordingly. Remain aware of the fact that in situations where persuasion plays a role, the choice rests with the other person.

26

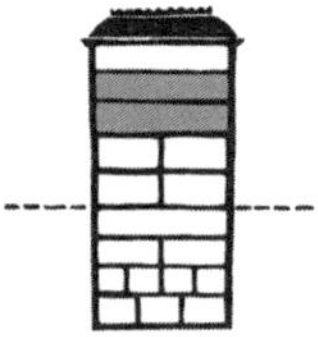

Negotiation (level +2 and +3)

This chapter gives a general introduction to negotiation techniques and the subjects of level +2 (value adding negotiations/problem solving) and level +3 (value sharing negotiations) of the winning dialogue system.

It is worth noting what a high position negotiation takes within the winning dialogue system. This might be interpreted in the following way: a good negotiation is dependent on several conditions. All parties involved must have a degree of willingness towards each other, information has to be exchanged, there has to be clarity about the conversation topics and – of utmost importance – there cannot be too much resistance, emotion or manipulation involved. These conditions are dealt with early on in the winning dialogue system. That means that there is often a lot of work to be done before negotiations can even begin. Another consequence of its position in the system is that the winning dialogue user must be alert to the need to temporarily interrupt negotiation in order to deal with issues on a lower level. If you as a reader have skipped ahead to this chapter, you ought to be aware that successful negotiators are not only sensitive to the need to switch to other conversation levels, but also master these one by one. They can all be viewed as an integral part of the process.

What constitutes good negotiation?

Many people think of intense conversations riddled with lies, aggression and manipulation when they picture negotiation. In my eyes, a negotiation does not have to be a struggle but in fact forms a constructive way to solve problems, come to agreements or share things fairly. Sometimes a collision cannot be prevented; often this type of escalation may even help your negotiation along. In other cases, you will have to reduce tension in order to turn your negotiation into a constructive process. A good winning dialogue negotiation is open and constructive and follows the principles outlined in chapter 1.

Negotiation comes in many forms, depending on the situation, the culture, the issues and the people involved. The winning dialogue system distinguishes between two forms of negotiation which each represent their own conversation level: value adding (level +2) and value sharing negotiations (level +3).

Value adding negotiations/problem solving

Value adding negotiation is a process where both parties are open to the other's interests, cooperate during the negotiation process and work towards mutually beneficial agreements. In this form of negotiation, the central idea is to search out each other's interests and alternatives with the goal of best serving both parties. For this reason, this approach is also suitable for solving problems. You will find more information about value adding negotiations/problem solving in chapter 29.

Value sharing negotiations

In value sharing negotiations both parties are focused on their own interests and thereby the results which they would like to achieve. The process does not have to be cooperative; you can encounter all sorts of strategies, tactics and techniques which your conversation partner may use to try and influence you in order for them to realize maximum profit. This 'harder' form of negotiation occupies level +3 of the winning dialogue system and will be addressed in chapter 30.

The negotiation situation

A negotiation situation is characterized by two elements: The parties involved must have a degree of dependence on one another and there must be a conflict of interests to some extent. An important distinction in negotiating behaviour which you can make based on these two elements is the distinction between 'fighting' and 'cooperating.' If you focus relatively more attention on the content, and therefore your own interests in the negotiation, you put your relationship with the other person in jeopardy (fighting). On the other hand: if you focus your attention on your interdependence and the relationship, you run the risk of losing sight of your own interests (cooperation).

As in other conversation situations, you and your conversation partner continually influence each other's behaviour: fighting behaviour provokes fighting behaviour and cooperative behaviour usually inspires cooperative behaviour. The latter is not always the case: you will have to match a challenging, fighting negotiator with a strong dose of firmness in order to prevent them from upsetting the process.

A general rule is that in situations where one party is fighting and the other is cooperating, the fighter will come out on top. Because of this, it may be necessary for a cooperative individual to (temporarily) also exhibit fighting behaviour while indicating if desired that they would prefer to negotiate in another way.

The complexity of negotiation can be illustrated with two games: the *prisoners' dilemma* and the *game of chicken* (Pruitt & Carnevale, 1993).

Prisoners' dilemma

In the prisoners' dilemma, two suspects of the same crime are locked up separately. They are both informed that they will receive one year in jail if they both confess. If they both deny the crime and are convicted, they will both receive five years in jail. If one confesses and one denies the crime, then the one who denies the crime will be released while the other one will receive 10 years in jail.

What is the smart thing to do in this situation? That depends on guessing what the other person will do. The person who denies the crime is in fact choosing for themselves because in that case the sentence is a maximum of five years, regardless of the other person's decision. Moreover, the person who denies the crime will be released should the other person confess. If you look at the issue from the point of view of both prisoners, a confession from both is the wisest option – the maximum punishment in this case is one year. The total time to be served by the prisoners in this case has a minimal value of two years as opposed to the ten years in all the other scenarios. Thus in fact, the two prisoners are working together to reach the best result for both (win-win).

The prisoners' dilemma shows that the result of cooperative behaviour depends on the other person's participation. If both suspects work together and can bank on that cooperation remaining intact, a best-case scenario (one year in jail for each) can be achieved for both of them. In the prisoners' dilemma fighting (denial) is less risky, but will never yield a positive result for both prisoners. The profit for the fighter – freedom – can only be had at the cost of the other prisoner, who will receive a more severe sentence – unless they also choose to fight.

In this scenario it is assumed that a win-win situation is possible and that both parties, as long as they work together, rather than fight, can benefit.

B / A	**Denial (fighting)**			**Confession (cooperation)**		
	A	**B**		**A**	**B**	
Denial (fighting)	5 years	5 years	Lose-lose	Free	10 years	Win - lose
Confession (cooperation)	10 years	Free	Win-lose	1 year	1 year	Win - Win

Table 1 Prisoners' dilemma: choices for parties A and B, and the situations these produce

An example of a prisoners' dilemma in day to day life is whether to lend books to colleagues.

It is better for me not to lend my books (fighting), because my colleagues may damage or lose them. As long as my colleagues still lend books to me, I am still ahead (win-lose). But if we no longer lend any books to each other we are worse off (lose-lose) than when we all borrow each other's books (win-win).

Game of chicken

Another, stranger, game is the game of chicken. In this game which was played by American teenagers in the fifties and sixties, two cars drive towards each other at top speed down the middle of the road. The one that swerves first loses. In this game there is never a win-win situation, because the only way to win the game is if the other person loses. In this case winning is not about trust but about credibility and commitment to a fighters' role. Whoever is capable of making the other person believe that he will drive on despite everything, has a good chance of winning. Naturally the most audacious player is counting on the other person to prefer losing the game to losing their life.

A \ B	**Swerve**	**Drive on**
Swerve	**lose - lose**	**lose - win**
Drive on	**win - lose**	**dead - dead**

Table 2 Game of chicken: choices for parties A and B, and the situations these produce

A game-of-chicken situation can easily crop up in real life if your negotiation partner confronts you with a tough demand which is in one way or another, conditional to the deal. As long as the deal is important enough to you, you will have to choose: do you accept the unfavourable condition (swerve) or do you stick to your guns (drive on). In the latter case you run the risk of the deal falling through.

An example of a game of chicken is the following situation:

You are occupied with trying to acquire a big new project as an independent organization advisor. Once the deal is almost signed and sealed, your client has a surprise for you: your rates have to go down by 25 percent otherwise the project will be cancelled. They would like to get your response tomorrow: yes or no.

Your performance	**Expected results**
Giving in to a tough demand	Retain deal under unfavourable conditions
Stick to your guns	Lose deal

Table 3 Game-of-chicken situation in practice

Examples of 'the prisoners' dilemma' and 'the game of chicken' come in all shapes and sizes in the day to day business world. In the first case, it pays to build trust and to look for opportunities for both parties to win. In the other case one party's win means the other party's loss. There are therefore different types of negotiation situations where different rules apply. This aspect is reflected in the distinction between value adding and value sharing negotiations (levels +2 and +3 respectively).

Looking at the negotiation process, value adding negotiation tends towards cooperation as in the prisoners' dilemma and a val-

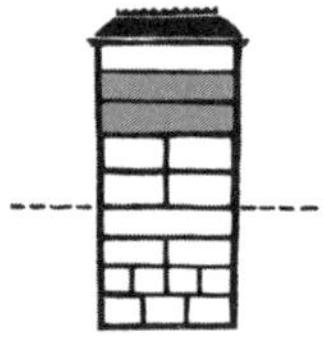

ue sharing negotiation towards fighting, as in the game of chicken. That does not take away from the fact that in both situations you and your conversation partner have to decide for yourselves if you wish to reach your goals through fighting or working together. This choice to work together or to fight must be clarified, because your negotiating style determines the successful interchange between you both. In all of these situations, it is important to be on your guard and not get bogged down in situations where you are not benefiting. That is why in a cooperative situation, such as value adding negotiations, you should not be too easily tempted into concessions. For value sharing negotiations the following applies: the fact that you have to stand up for your own interests and it can get rough, does not have to lead to an impossible posture or an icy atmosphere.

The dilemma between cooperating and fighting, in combination with the high stakes that can be involved in a negotiation, makes negotiation the most complex part of communication. In a negotiation situation everything is up for discussion, even the discussion itself.

The conflict spiral

In principle, you achieve the best results in negotiation if you and the other person are prepared to work together in looking for a solution that is mutually beneficial (a win-win situation). If the situation is tense or if the relationship between you is not strong enough and the stakes are high, then a negotiation will tend towards fighting. As the atmosphere becomes more contentious, you will both focus more on your own interests and the desired results, without examining the consequences for the other person (a win-lose situation). A conflict can get so heated that both parties lean towards a situation where they inflict damage on the other, even at the cost of their own interests (a lose-lose situation). That brings them into a conflict spiral (see figure 1), which is comparable to the circle of resistance in chapter 16.

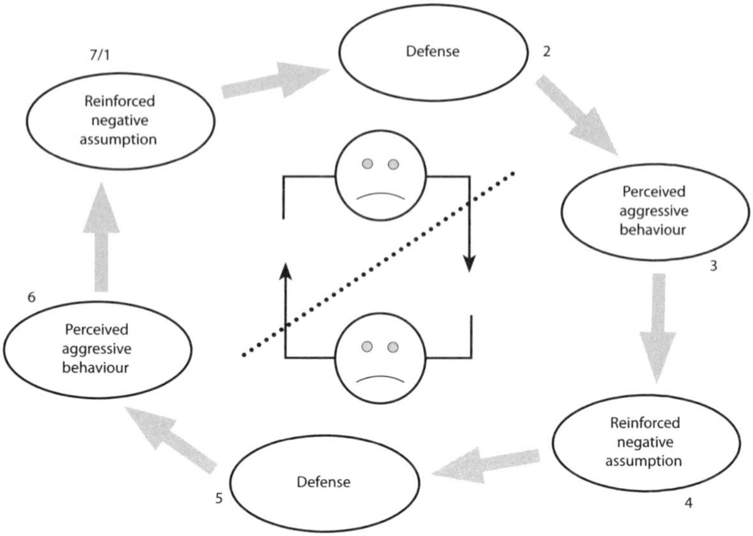

Figure 1 The conflict spiral (source: Ryan & Oestreich, 1991)

As tension increases, so does the likelihood of a lose-lose situation, as seen in figure 2. The greater the degree of tension, the more the parties involved are prone to accept bad results as long as it adversely affects the other as well.

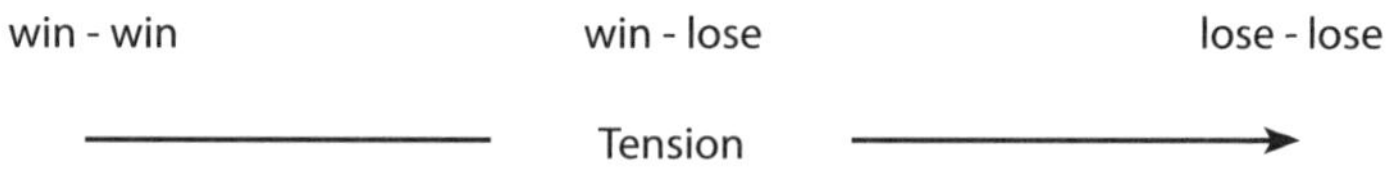

Figure 2 Shifting of negotiation goals due to increasing tension

To avoid getting bogged down in a situation where negotiations turn out badly for one or both parties, it is important to continually fos-

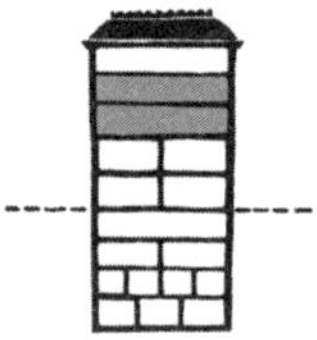

ter a good relationship with the other party and to limit the degree of conflict involved in the negotiation (Mastenbroek, 1996). That is why it is so essential to shift to lower conversation levels in the winning dialogue system, when necessary, in order to preserve and maintain the basis for your negotiation. If for example emotion, manipulation or resistance come up, you will benefit from dealing with these issues on the appropriate level before you continue with negotiations. If you do not do so, you run the risk of the negotiation escalating and ending up as a conflict which is difficult to resolve.

There are a number of books which have been written about negotiation which go into detail about how you can deal with the dilemma of fighting versus cooperating. Perhaps the most important conclusion which can be gleaned from these is that it is actually a false dilemma; namely, it is possible to promote your interests while at the same time fostering a good relationship with the other party. In other words: you can be tough handling the problem at hand and tender with the people involved (Fisher & Ury, 1994).

Negotiation as a zero sum game

In addition to the pitfall of placing too much emphasis on either cooperation or fighting, there is another big risk in negotiation: the tendency people have to focus too much on one or only a few aspects of the final agreement. This often limits negotiation to a restricted area which decreases the possibility of a win-win result for the conversation partners. The reason why people negotiate this way stems from an assumption that the results of a negotiation must have the same value for each party; the cost of a concession by one must be equal in value to what this provides for the other. People see negotiation as a *zero sum game*. The game of chicken is a perfect zero sum game as long as both parties swerve: the profit of one is equal to the loss of the other.

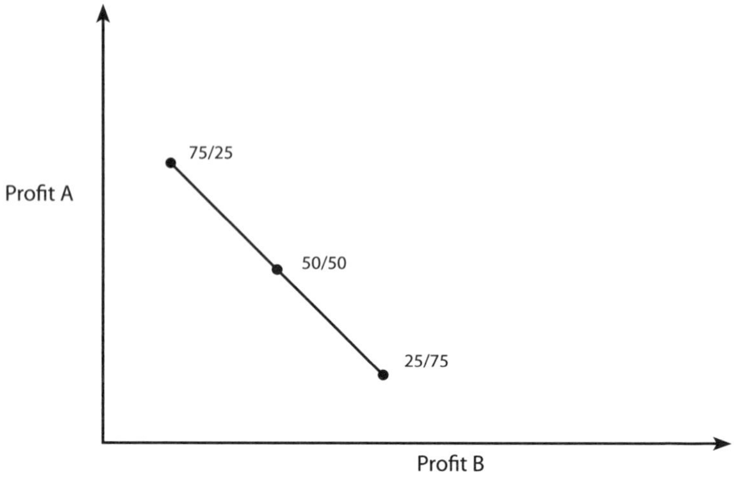

Figure 3 Negotiation as a zero sum game: what A loses, B wins (benefit to B) – and vice versa; the sum remains the same: the process of negotiation does not create extra value

The relatively simple idea of a zero sum game actually creates no extra value for either party. The basis for a real win-win situation lies in the fact that the negotiating parties assign a different value to specific negotiation results or through their cooperation increase the value of the sum of individual contributions. For a miller with a large supply of flour, the cost of conceding a few kilos of free flour is relatively low, while the value of this concession is of great worth to a baker who does not have enough flour. This is the core of the 'enlarging the pie' idea (value adding negotiations), a way to escape zero sum games.

As I said: people often assume they are dealing with a zero sum game. But if they take the trouble to look a bit further, they will discover all sorts of other possibilities. That is why it's important to test the zero sum assumption and to examine if there is more to negotiate on than originally thought. Think about alternatives and be creative!

Negotiation as a positive sum game

By examining possibilities to generate extra value for you and your negotiation partner in an inventive manner, you create a *positive sum game*. Since money often, though not always, has the same value for both parties (and can therefore be a real zero sum game),* the space for negation can usually be found in other issues. It is therefore crucial to be alert about other possible issues during negotiation and also to look at what other factors might play a role in enlarging the pie. If you are aware of this and work towards it, you shift the profit line in figure 4 to the top right and together with your negotiation partner you create extra value which would not be there without joint negotiation. Based on this extra profit, it is often easier for both parties to come to a mutually satisfactory result.

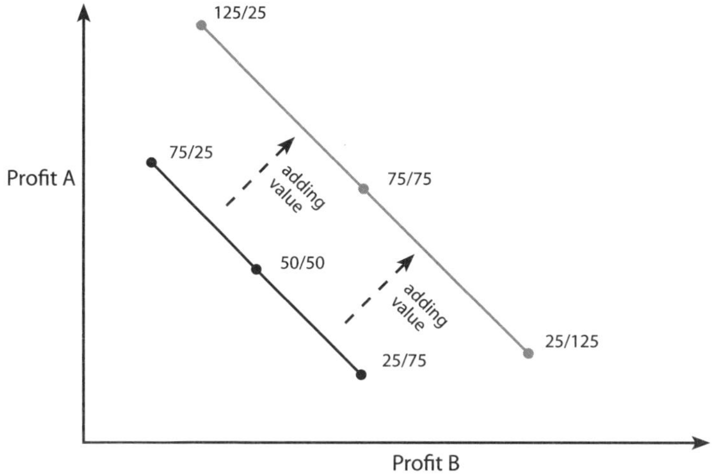

Figure 4 Negotiation as a positive sum game increases the total sum (value adding negotiations) and shifts the line up; both parties can increase their profit or benefit and create a win-win situation

** In practice, the value of money is seen differently by individual parties. For example if a HR staff member is negotiating a severance payment with an employee on behalf of the company, for understandable reasons, both parties look at the money involved very differently.*

The process of looking for extra value is known as *exploration*. The position exploration has in a negotiation is partially determined by the negotiation style. The winning dialogue system distinguishes two: value adding and value sharing negotiations. In value adding negotiations, mutual exploration plays a central role, while this is not true of negotiations focused on value sharing. In the next chapter the skills of exploration will be outlined in detail.

Chapters 27 and 28 address general skills for negotiators and the preparation for negotiations according to the winning dialogue system. After which follows a detailed explanation of value adding and value sharing negotiations in chapters 29 and 30.

27

Skills for negotiators

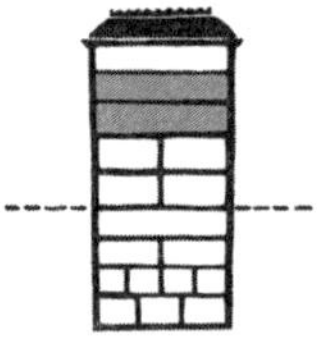

Negotiation is a complex process. Negotiations are dynamic and sometimes confusing because different issues can come up at the same time. Short forays to other conversation levels are often necessary. To bring order to the chaos, when discussing negotiation I distinguish four skill areas which you will often use as a negotiator and which are related to other winning dialogue levels:

- Exploring (+1A)
- Persuading (+1B, -1)
- Influencing the process (0)
- Setting limits (-3)

Exploring

Exploration is about uncovering information relating to mutual interests, investigating room for negotiation and testing alternatives. Exploring is something you do primarily by listening, watching for (non-verbal) signals and asking sharp questions. There is an important relationship between exploring and level +1 (listening/receiving information). During negotiation it is important to look at the motives and interests underlying the position being taken. By figuring this out, you can make room to reach a satisfactory solution from an initial, seemingly irreconcilable position.

The use of 'test balloons' can be helpful in discovering how your conversation partner views a certain solution, alternative or concession, but also how much value they assign to the various topics which play a role in your negotiation. A test balloon is an option launched by you which you invite the other person to respond to and often takes the form of an alternative solution or a conditional concession.

If you use a test balloon, you must ensure that you do not make it concrete, so not: 'If..., then...', but: 'Say that..., how/what would you then...?' Because if you are too explicit, the other person can see your test balloon as a concrete proposal and respond directly, which commits you to it. To avoid this, it is a good idea to literally announce your test balloon for what it is.

To find out how fixed your conversation partner's position is, you can move to a 'harder' style of exploration. In this case, you up the pressure by presenting an ambitious demand, by reacting negatively to a proposition or by increasing the time pressure. For example, if you, as a buyer, indicate that the order will not go through because the price is too high, the salesperson will have to stand very firm if they do not want to give up his possible negotiating room.

Persuading

In negotiation situations, persuasion comes down to presenting your ideas and positions to the other person so that they are acceptable and favourable. That means that you constantly have to think about your conversation partner's position and interests. The better able you are to link your proposal to their interests, the greater the chance that they will be agreeable and accept your proposition. If you have to make concessions, do not forget to articulate the value of such, if possible, from their perspective. As small as a concession may seem in your eyes, it may mean a lot to your conversation partner – and vice versa of course.

It is not a good idea to mention too many arguments: a few strong arguments work best here as well. Always be prepared for a negative reaction. If this should come up, then you can shift back to the resistance level (-1). A good response to resistance can greatly increase your powers of persuasion. Additionally, you can gain insight into your conversation partner's value system, concerns and considerations (exploration), which will help you to better formulate your arguments and proposals to suit him.

Influencing the process

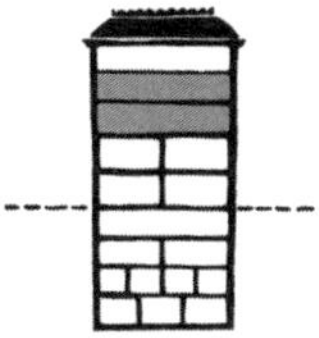

Aspects such as the sequence in which various subjects will be addressed and whether they are discussed separately or as a whole, can greatly influence the course and result of negotiations. An unstructured negotiation process does not improve the effectiveness of your negotiation. Practiced negotiators understand the value of the agenda and the process to be negotiation tools, and will attempt to use these to exert influence. In the winning dialogue system there is a conversation level specially focused on influencing the process in conversations: the introducing structure level. Since the theory about this is relevant to the effectiveness of negotiation, I advise you to carefully read through chapters 19 and 20.

In some negotiations you may have to deal with negotiations about the negotiation. In which case both parties have their own ideas about how the conversation should go and are not prepared to deviate. Intervening in the process can be necessary if the negotiation itself becomes the subject of negotiation, if your chosen route turns out not to be the right one, or during confusion or conflicts. If you need a break, if you need time to think or want to schedule a moment when you can separate generating ideas from deciding about ideas, an intervention in the process is a good idea.

Setting limits

In negotiation, beyond content related limits, you can also set two other types of limits: restoring the balance of power and preventing challenging behaviour.

Content related limits

In a certain sense, negotiations only arise if it is explicitly clear that you and your conversation partner are not in (immediate) agreement. If you listen to a proposition which is unacceptable to you without reacting, the other person will assume that they have got a foot in the door. You then have to fight your way out of an uncomfortable position. You can help yourself, your conversation partner and the negotiation process by being clear and direct: indicate in a brief, clear, but friendly manner that the proposal as it now stands is unacceptable to you. In this context, unacceptability can be determined by limits to your mandate, by your points of resistance or by a better BATNA.* After you have done so, it is better not to allow long silences or give the other person a lot of space to protest. Rather, proceed immediately to indicate what can be discussed and take the initiative to bring the negotiation back to a constructive interaction.

Restoring the balance of power

During negotiations a certain balance of power is extremely important. If it is disturbed too much, it becomes difficult to come to a negotiation process – let alone an acceptable result for both of you. If what your conversation partner does or says gives you the feeling that the balance of power is being upset, then you need to take action to restore it.

Your conversation partner can attempt different things, for example:

- Establishing their own position of power by emphasizing their independence from you
- Forcefully and without consultation influencing the negotiation process or circumstances
- Limiting your freedom of choice in any way

Negotiations are conducted in principle by free people who choose to come to an agreement. And although utilizing that freedom is not without consequences, it is important that you realize that you are free to determine your own behaviour. This freedom can even lead

**'BATNA' stands for 'Best Alternative to a Negotiated Agreement.' See chapter 29 for more.*

to you breaking off negotiations. With this knowledge in mind, it is important that you stay in touch with your feelings over the course of your negotiation. Your feelings indicate when something is off in the balance of power. Should you, no matter how subtle, hear a remark or observe behaviour that is aimed at upsetting the balance of power, react with appropriate firmness and subtlety. If you can manage it, a humorous response is an excellent way to restore the balance.

Preventing challenging behaviour

If your conversation partner works against you, manipulates you or negatively influences you in other ways, it will stand in the way of a positive result from the negotiation. That is why it is important to put aside the content of your negotiation and focus on your conversation partner's behaviour for a time. If their behaviour irritates you and interrupts the negotiation process, you can do something about it by moving to level -3 (hidden opposition and influence). Another intervention which applies to this specific situation is called *controlled decontrolling*: you identify the behaviour which is bothering you and articulate what emotions it inspires in you. But do not get carried away by the emotions! For example, you say that a certain remark upsets you rather than bursting out with rage. It is important in doing so that you only identify the emotion and do not add in non-verbal extras, such as crossing your arms, raising your voice or proverbially pounding your fist on the table, because that will only escalate the situation anyway.

28

Preparation for negotiation

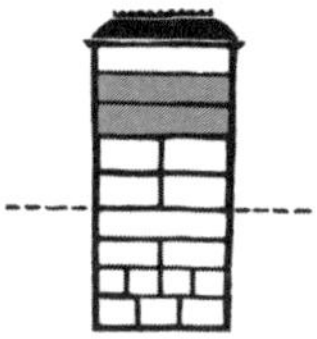

In chapter 3 you find general information about the preparation for conversations based on the winning dialogue system. Three preparatory steps are outlined therein: an analysis of the situation, setting goals and choosing an approach. If you expect your conversation to involve a great deal of negotiation, it is worth the trouble to consider the following three points in your preparation as well:

- The content
- Your strategy
- The information

The content

The content of each negotiation hinges on matters about which agreements must be made during the negotiation. In the theory of this book, these matters or subjects are known as *issues*. Issues with buying a car can be: the price, extra accessories, the delivery time, financing possibilities, the trade-in price of your current car and warranty guarantees. Possible solutions are relevant on the value adding negotiations/problem solving level as well as the value sharing negotiations level. They are based on a combination of positions on the various issues, acceptable concessions and the willingness to take another position on one or more issues. Before you begin negotiating, it is good to know what issues will be addressed and to think about the question of how issues can be redirected in the interests of both parties. A position on an issue represents another value for each party, and the better able you are to gauge that value, the stronger your negotiation will be.

In their book *Getting to Yes,* Fisher and Ury (1994) introduce the phenomenon of 'principled negotiation', as part of the Harvard negotiation project. Principled negotiation, called 'value adding negotiation' in the winning dialogue system, stands for a way of negotiating in which interests are exchanged based on their value for each of the individual negotiators. In contrast to this is 'positional negotiation' ('value sharing negotiation'), in which the pie is shared by giving and taking bit by bit.

Value adding negotiations (more about this in the next chapter) can best be prepared for by assessing your interests and those of your negotiation partner to the best of your ability. From there, think about what your BATNA (more about this in the next chapter as well) is and what issues are relevant to you. Establish what you would like to accomplish regarding these issues. Watch out that you are not too rigid in value adding negotiations; that may threaten your creativity during the conversation.

During negotiations of a sharing nature (see chapter 30) it is wise to make the issues relevant to you and the results you hope to achieve more concrete for your conversation partner. Before you begin the conversation, try to determine your target points and points of resistance on the most important issues. Your target point is the most ambitious position you can defend and your resistance point indicates the minimum level at which an agreement is acceptable to you. During your negotiation, try and come out as close as possible to your target point; your opening offer will usually be based on this, because that offer is always the most ambitious. Research into negotiation has proven that people who start high achieve higher results on average. Be advised, 'high' has to be realistically high, because if you start unreasonably high your negotiation partner will not take you seriously. You have to be able to defend your opening offer with reasonable arguments. Usually, various issues are discussed at the same time in a negotiation. In this sense, think about combinations of positions on the various issues. The target and resistance points then become target and resistance packages.

It is wise to have these clearly outlined before the start of your negotiation so that you have a guideline for yourself. Often a negotiation becomes complex so quickly that there is no time to think while you are talking. Moreover, you are less vulnerable to all sorts of manipulative techniques if you have a guideline.

To ensure that you can defend your positions, your prices and your conditions during a negotiation, I recommend you prepare for these as well. Make sure that you know all your arguments and try to imagine your conversation partner's arguments so that you can think about your reaction to them. Also try to anticipate possible objections to your proposal. If you have difficulty with this, it can help to put yourself in the other person's shoes and consider what you would say if the other person presented you with your proposal.

Your strategy

If you prepare for a negotiation, you have to think about its course. How do you want to play the game? The duration and the sequence in which the issues are discussed and decided on, and the timing of providing information are quite important.

As for the sequence in which issues are addressed, you have the most influence if you begin the opening with an agenda proposal. Indicate which topic you would like to begin with and how you would like to continue. In order to increase the likelihood that your conversation partner will accept your agenda, it is a good idea to present their interests in your proposal. It is also wise to determine beforehand when you want to submit your opening offer. Some negotiators prefer to let the other party make an opening offer and thus protect themselves against the risk of presenting an offer which is too low. Others like to make the first hit and thus strengthen their own position.

If you are working on a value sharing negotiation, then it is a good idea to decide which concessions you are willing to make and at what point – and what you would like to get in return.

If you are negotiating as a team, the controversies within your team must be eliminated to the extent possible before the negotiation so

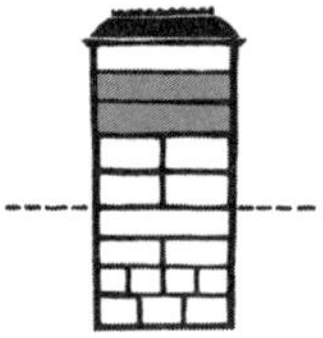

that you can work with one goal and one strategy. It helps to appoint a leader within the team to do the lion's share of the talking. Others can then contribute based on their agreed role. Make sure that you have clear arrangements for as many issues as possible prior to beginning negotiations as a team. And agree that, should the negotiation take an unexpected turn or the team members need it, a time-out will be requested.

With your posture and attitude during the negotiation, you determine for your part the atmosphere and therefore also the way in which you would like to come to an agreement. Do you want to create an atmosphere of trust or is it important to show your fangs? Should it be a cool, professional atmosphere or would a warm, open atmosphere be more to your advantage?

One last point regarding your strategy is the manner in which you wish to communicate with your negotiation partner prior to the negotiation. You can namely exert a good deal of influence on their perception of the available negotiating room beforehand.

Information: know what you don't know

In negotiating, it is very important that you are aware of the reliability of the information that you have – and obtain. Most negotiations are conducted based on mutual assumptions. This is not bad in and of itself, as long as you are aware of it. Examine the source of every bit of information you have used in making your preparation. Is it a fact or an assumption? And if it is an assumption, what might you have to do before or during the negotiation to test it? A good preparation on this point, in combination with alertness during the negotiation, can reveal a treasure trove of information which you can use to strengthen your position. Vice versa, it is also wise to examine if assumptions are playing a role with your negotiation partner and thus influencing the negotiation as a whole.

29

Level +2: value adding negotiations/problem solving

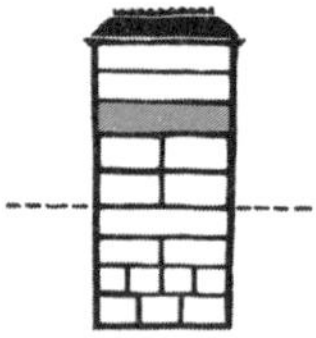

On this level, despite an initial difference in point of view, you work together with your negotiation partner to find mutually beneficial solutions so that both parties can achieve an optimal result. Value adding negotiations are also known as 'principled negotiations'. What then is the principle? The most important is that during a value adding negotiation both parties work towards achieving a good deal for each other. In his book *The Eighth Habit,* Covey (2005) calls this principle 'win-win or no deal'. Both parties are working under the assumption that they are free to close a deal – or not. A deal is only closed if it is advantageous for both parties.

The lead-up to a negotiation situation is a combination of divergent interests and mutual dependence. We will assume that, if you have arrived at this level, you have exchanged information and that there has been a proposal made which you and your negotiation partner have not yet reached a consensus on. You still have divergent positions and it is not entirely clear to what extent your interests overlap. On this conversation level you will examine each other's interests in order to come up with a solution which is acceptable for both parties.

Practical tips

What is the difference between value adding negotiations and value sharing negotiations? In my view it comes down to the basics: rather than looking out for number one, value adding negotiators are looking for a fair solution for all parties involved. They are concerned with interests and not with positions, as value sharing negotiators are. This can be expressed with the different tools for principled negotiators (Fisher & Ury, 1994):

- Talk about interests rather than positions
- Think of alternatives which are mutually beneficial
- View 'conceptualizing' and 'deciding' as two different processes
- Focus on objective criteria and a fair deal for all parties involved
- Develop your BATNA

Talk about interests rather than positions

A position is a solution to a problem which one party would like to see accepted and is characterized by being static. Your positions are in fact previously established solutions which you have chosen because they serve your interests. The question is whether there are other solutions which might serve your interests just as well or even better, because they certainly exist. There are countless solutions to the same problem. Everything centres on interests – things which matter to both parties in the most favourable scenario. An example:

As the person responsible for personnel policy, you like to think about the future. In order to ensure sufficient quality in the future, you would like to strengthen the training programs in your organization and attract more young, recently graduated talent. You expect that this will cost 35,000 euro annually. So in a board meeting you present your position that your budget should be increased by this amount. Your proposal is waved away by other board members with the argument that they could also make improvements if they had extra resources. Subsequently, everyone presents their personal position and the meeting bogs down in a never ending discussion. The result: no solution.

If you had focused on interests in your presentation, such as strengthening the organization for the future and having talented staff available, other board members might have discovered that their interests overlapped yours and you could have worked together to find creative solutions which are logical and helpful to everyone.

It is up to you to ensure that your negotiation partner understands and acknowledges your interests. And you in turn have to understand their interests and give them a place in the negotiation. That is easy to combine: you will note that if you acknowledge the interests of the other person, they will be prepared to acknowledge yours.

Think of alternatives which are mutually beneficial

While negotiators in value sharing negotiations come together by 'haggling'*, in value adding negotiations you and your negotiation parter investigate alternatives and focus on solutions which are beneficial to you both. Investigating alternatives can help to clarify which interests are being represented. With your negotiation partner, you can investigate multiple alternatives (at the same time). An important advantage of this is that you will start to think more freely and come up with ideas that you never would have thought of on your own. Moreover, solutions which are thought up *together* on the spot will have the greatest likelihood of acceptance by you both.

View 'thinking' and 'deciding' as two separate processes

Experience teaches us that it is very difficult to think creatively about alternatives if all parties are involved in tough negotiations and every word counts. Fear and lack of trust produce a stressful atmosphere. For most people, tension inhibits the information exchange, the thought process and the 'ping ponging' of ideas. That is why it is a good idea to do as much thinking and exploring as is possible beforehand, and to make explicit agreements about the question whether 'every word counts' or if ideas may be freely tossed around. Since this latter point can help the different players to best merge their ideas, it is important not only to make agreements about the course of the conversation (the agenda), but also about the weight that is given to comments made in the heat of the moment.

** The process of 'haggling' involves you slowly but surely moving from your initial position while your negotiation partner manoeuvres in your direction little by little.*

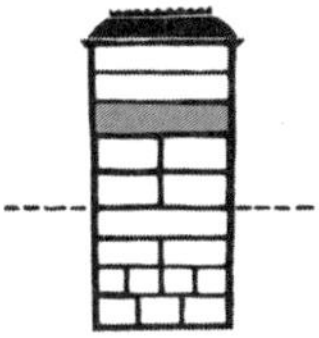

Focus on objective criteria and a fair deal for all parties involved

Naturally, as a value adding negotiator you cannot avoid the moment when a price must be agreed on or another value has to be shared. At some point, you have to get down to business and then exploring comes to an end. In doing so, you will try and approach the issue from your interests as well as those of your negotiation partner so that the sharing can be fair, transparent and acceptable to you both. Externally verified criteria which are acceptable for both parties and which assess the fairness of alternative solutions (for example, opinions of external experts, valuations, suggested prices and market information), are essential to this. A true value adding negotiator will reject any form of 'haggling' and demand that sharing be based on mutually acceptable, objective criteria.

If both parties have a good feeling about the negotiated results, it benefits the relationship. Some people think this is only important to a long term relationship; if you are involved in a onetime deal then the relationship does not matter much. But during a negotiation, you have no idea how the relationship with your conversation partner may develop in the future and in what way you may become dependent on this person or their opinion of you. Broken trust is difficult to recover and your reputation is worth more than any individual negotiation result.

Develop your BATNA

Where a value sharing negotiator chooses a point of resistance, the value adding negotiator thinks about the BATNA (Best Alternative to a Negotiated Agreement). Simply put, the BATNA stands for what you can get somewhere else. This means that you look for alternative solutions which lie outside the ongoing negotiation in case you cannot work it out with your negotiation partner. The advantage of a good BATNA is that you thereby increase your position in the negotiation. Your dependence on the other person decreases as does your likelihood of accepting a relatively uninteresting proposal. In extreme cases, in order to increase the pressure somewhat, you can carefully confront your negotiation partner with your BATNA and the price they may pay for negotiating too ambitiously.

For example, if you want to sell your house and are negotiating with party A, the bid by party B is your BATNA. You can always choose to accept this rather than move forward with party A.

Advantages and disadvantages of the value adding approach

A value adding way of negotiating is a great way to negotiate. In complex negotiations with high stakes and many interests involved, this method will produce the best results in most cases. But it is not an easy way. Opposite a hard as stone negotiation partner it can be tricky to use the value adding approach. If you are more of a value adding negotiator and your conversation partner is a positional negotiator, it can be difficult to get them to go along with the value adding process.

In routine or one dimensional (price) negotiations where the relationship between the parties is relatively unimportant (for example, the buying and selling of houses), a value adding negotiation provides little extra value and it can save time to come to a value sharing agreement by haggling.

Examples

Moving a positional discussion to a discussion of interests

Position of a personnel manager in an employment contract conversation:

'You can see that I'm reluctant about the salary you are requesting. That is because others in our organization are compensated within the framework of the wage scale which I outlined for you. I would be causing trouble and above all increasing costs if I were to meet your demands.'

Position of an applicant in an employment contract conversation:
'I feel that salary is an important point because I worry that once I am pigeonholed I will never get out of that wage scale. I also feel that in the long run I will provide significant added value for this organization and I would like to receive fitting remuneration for that.'

Inviting others to move from positions to interests:

- 'I can tell that salary is a difficult issue for you, what are your underlying motives?'
- 'What does the initial salary mean for you?'
- 'What exactly will you do with 35,000 euro for training and attracting new talent?'
- 'Say we follow through with your request, what concrete results will that produce for the organization?'

Practical tips

Distinguishing 'thinking' from 'deciding':
'At this time we are pretty far apart. Shall we – without reading into each other's words – see if we can think up some creative alternatives which are mutually beneficial? Then we can see which alternatives are best for both of us.'

Objective criteria:

- 'I do not want to just agree to any price for the trade-in. Shall we take a look at the Auto Club used car prices and base our decision on that?'
- 'What is an objective criterion we can use to decide which distribution is fair to us both?'

Fair deal:
'I am not sure if this solution serves your interests or mine, but I think it is important that we leave the table with a good solution and a satisfied feeling.'

Confrontation with the BATNA:

- 'I see that our conversation is not making much progress. If we do not work it out together, I will seriously look into the other buyer's bid.'
- 'If we cannot reach an agreement on an, in my opinion, fair salary, then I will have to enter negotiations with employers who have a different view of things.'

Next steps

If you can get your conversation partner to cooperate in a value adding negotiation, you will undoubtedly achieve results. If you have worked everything out, move on to the wrapping up and closing deals level. If there are any points concerning sharing left to discuss, you can do so on the value sharing negotiations level.

Difficulty with value adding negotiations/problem solving?

For people who have difficulty with this conversation level, the following pitfalls can play a role:

- Belief in a hard fighting style
- Difficulty putting yourself in the other person's place
- Fear of losing
- Little trust in the other person
- Lack of personal strength

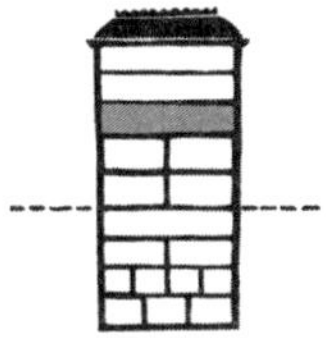

Belief in a hard fighting style

If you are convinced that a good negotiation should be an all out fight, you will develop a tough negotiating style. Your negotiation partners will react to that with a similar posture, with the consequence that the negotiation will turn into a fight very quickly. Your conviction is strengthened by observation, which will only seem to justify your tough style even more.

Difficulty putting yourself in the other person's place

It can be tough to create an overview of your own interests and those of your conversation partner and then to translate your position into their interests. Some people have difficulty looking at a negotiation situation from the other party's point of view. Is that true for you too? Then it would help if you prepare for your negotiations with someone you trust who can play the part of the other party. Other than that, putting yourself in the other person's position is a question of experience. By consciously working on it, it will become easier for you to do.

Fear of losing

It may be that you are worried about the fact that you might not get a lot out of a negotiation situation. That can make you rigid; out of safety considerations, you refuse to deviate from your position. If you still want to negotiate by adding value, I advise you to put your fears aside, make conscious choices you can live with and make an effort to negotiate constructively. Answering the question as to why you are afraid of losing can help you to release your worries – which will help you negotiate in a much more effective way.

Little trust in the other person

The trust you have in your conversation partner plays an important role in carrying out negotiations. If this area leaves much to be desired, then try and set aside your lack of trust and concentrate as much as possible on the negotiation process. A smooth negotiation can contribute to a restoration of trust in the other person. Be realistic about it and stay in touch with your feelings: your distrust might be well founded. If you really think that your negotiation partner is untrustworthy, take a look at an appropriate BATNA and consider breaking off the negotiation. In any case, make sure you have clear agreements that are easy to check.

Lack of personal strength

Although value adding negotiations may seem like the path of least resistance, to use this technique you need quite a lot of personal strength because standing up for your interests is not always easy. This is especially true if you are negotiating with someone who would prefer to negotiate in another manner. You then have to consciously stick to your way of working and be prepared to link possible consequences to any abuse of your method.

Strength in your personal performance is rooted in personality and experience – aspects which in the short term you can have little influence on. What you can influence is the degree to which you consciously choose to defend your interests. A well thought out choice creates clarity for yourself. If you know for certain what you want and what is important to you, you will come across as much stronger and more forceful than when you are still in doubt.

30

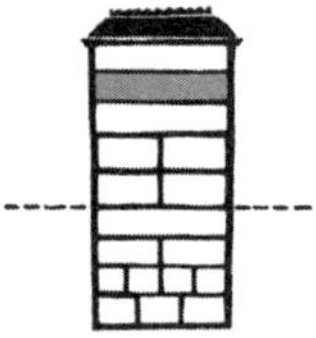

Level +3: value sharing negotiations

The type of negotiation which produces the best results in terms of business and relationships is value adding negotiation. That is why it is a good idea to try and reach a win-win situation in this manner in every negotiation. But that is not always possible: sometimes opposing interests remain on this level even after you have examined ways to merge your interests. Sometimes a negotiation situation does not lend itself to a value adding approach, for example, if you are dealing with a hard as stone negotiation partner. In these cases, you are referred to a value sharing negotiation.

Just as with value adding negotiations, exploring is a big part of this type of negotiation because it might turn out that the deal can be closed in a value adding manner after all. Some possibilities for exploring enlargement of the pie only become visible when negotiators are engaged in tough negotiations. Should points of negotiation not actually lend themselves to a value adding solution, then these points must be brought to a mutually acceptable conclusion through value sharing.

In value sharing negotiations, you and your negotiation partner both take up a starting position. This starting position – your opening offer – should be on the ambitious side because you are both assuming it will have to be diluted somewhat. The subsequent negotiation is a process of haggling: through small concessions, you both move closer and closer to one another. If everything goes well, you will eventually end up at a point somewhere in the middle which is acceptable to you both. The price of houses and cars are usually agreed upon with this type of negotiation.

Practical tips

The process of value sharing negotiation is, especially if you are dealing with hardened negotiators, not easy and full of pitfalls. The art is to play this negotiation game in a calm way, without losing your alertness. The following tips will help increase your chances of succeeding.

Opening Move

Value sharing negotiations are usually introduced with an 'opening move' in which the negotiation partners get a sense of each other, research the issues and explore the negotiation situation. Subsequently they make it clear to one another through their opening offer that they each have different interests in resolving the issue at hand and establish the fact that they have more or less divergent positions. Each negotiator then defends the reasonableness of their starting offer and indicates that they would not be happy with another solution. If both parties still oppose one another in this way for too long without budging, it is likely that the negotiation will be prematurely ended or that a conflict will arise. In order to avoid this, negotiators signal that they are willing to shift their position, as long as the other person is also prepared to do so. Sending and receiving these types of messages is a signal for both sides to start making concessions.

Concession strategy

During the opening move it became clear that your initial positions seem irreconcilable. If all went well, you have also let each other know that you are willing to make concessions. Through your concessions, you will both now attempt to merge your position and eventually reach an agreement somewhere halfway between the initial standpoints. Ambitious negotiators will do their best using smart concessions to ensure that their results in the negotiation process are a little better than average. A few tips:

- Sketch a detailed picture for yourself of what you can offer and what might be valuable to the other person. Consider the smallest details: even planning the negotiation in a certain place or at a certain time can be of value. Remember that each proposal you go along with which is valuable to the other person can be thought of as a concession.

- Gather as much value for your negotiation partner as you can before you begin negotiations. Use creative thinking to come up with things you can bring to the table which are valuable for them. For example, when purchasing new cars for our staff we prefer not to buy one at a time, but two or three. That way we increase the value of the transaction for the car dealer and we can ask for larger discounts.
- During your negotiation, look for concessions which are easy for you to give away and are valuable to the other party. These so-called low cost, high benefit concessions, which can lead to extra value for both parties, stem from the idea that not all aspects have the same value for all parties. Think about the miller and the baker in the paragraph 'negotiation as a zero sum game' in chapter 26 for example.
- If you make concessions during value sharing negotiations, never give something away for which you get nothing in return. A concession always has to be made conditionally because if you do not do so, you run the risk that your negotiation partner will say 'thank you' and you will not get anything in return. Practiced negotiators use cunning techniques to trump people who forget to use the principle of conditional concessions. Always allow the principle of conditional concessions to sink in and be on guard for every situation where there is no direct connection between a concession from your side – of whatever kind – and one in return from your negotiation partner.
- Watch the timing of your concessions. A specific concession can have relatively little impact in the beginning of a negotiation while it might put the other person over the line at the end of

a warm Friday afternoon or when a plane must be caught. On the other hand, you can increase your negotiation partner's irritation and distrust if you wait too long in making concessions on important points. To prevent that, it can be a good idea to trade big concessions early on in the negotiation. A general statement about the right timing cannot be made. You will have to determine for yourself which concession will have the most impact at which time, depending on your estimation of the situation and the interests of the other person.

End game

If you are close to reaching an agreement, the end game begins. The rule applies here as well: give nothing away without obtaining something in return. If everything goes according to plan, an important concession – definitive consent to the deal – is in sight in the end game. If you want to sell something or are trying to persuade someone, agreement is the important concession you are looking for. In fact, that concession means relinquishing freedom, the freedom to change opinions or to go and look elsewhere. With the finish line in sight, you run the risk of making the agreement more attractive to the other person, without actually closing the deal. If you do not link your last concessions with reaching an agreement, you run the risk of reducing the value of the deal without actually getting it. You also open yourself up to the 'higher power' trick (more about this later, in the paragraph 'negotiation tricks'), which the other person can use to get one more concession out of you. Reversed: if you want to buy something or someone is trying to persuade you, then your definitive consent is the ultimate concession from your side which can usually earn you something. The key to a good end game is that both parties simultaneously come to an agreement which exploits the *low cost, high benefit* principle to the maximum and which produces the greatest returns for both parties.

Issue management

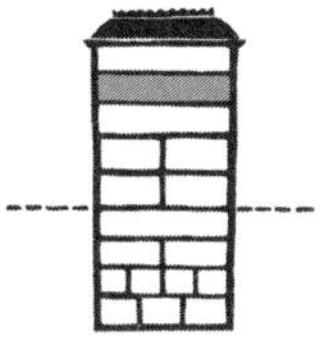

In every negotiation, you will have to make deals about various issues. In commercial transactions these may include the price, the quality, the delivery time, the logistics or the packaging. For each of these points, myriad solutions might be chosen. Insight into the relevant issues, their relationship to one another and the relative value of each is important in a good value sharing negotiation. If prior to the negotiation you have thought about the question of how the issues can be traded against each other, then you can deal with a sharing issue creatively. This is especially important in complex negotiation situations.

Issues are interesting because:

- They can help you determine the range of the negotiation
- You can use them to increase or decrease the complexity of the negotiation
- Every party assigns different (relative) interests to them
- Every party has different target and resistance points on the various issues

If you know how to handle issues cleverly and creatively, not only can you best exploit the exploration opportunities in a negotiation, you are also capable of influencing the nature of the negotiation game. Certainly during intense negotiations with tough conversation partners you can gain crucial advantages in this way.

If too many issues are being discussed at the same time, it can be helpful to decrease the range of the negotiation. For example, in a negotiation about the purchase of various products you can suggest bundling the individual issues to simplify the negotiation process. In this case you are talking about one discount percentage rather than about different prices. Another possibility is to 'park' certain issues and first focus on solving priority issues.

If a negotiation gets bogged down, you can split the issues, bring up new issues or reactivate parked issues. In this way you ensure that the new talking points create the necessary room to progress.

When trading issues during a negotiation, I prefer not to work with concrete concessions which tie me down and move me farther away from my starting position. Rather, I try to find alternative possibilities for our individual positions on various issues. By playing with the various issues creatively, I can look at a negotiation from different sides and shape the game into a form that suits me. An effective issue manager can launch alternatives at the drop of hat, trading one issue for another. Make sure that if you are going to play with the issues, you have an accurate picture of the value of each issue. If you don't have a sufficient grasp of the relative importance of all the relevant issues, you have a significant chance of losing!

Returning from conflict to negotiation

The underlying principle of value sharing negotiation is that both parties take an ambitious starting position and subsequently move towards one another slowly but surely via all sorts of detours. In reality, this is not always the case. In order to conduct a value sharing negotiation effectively, both parties must know the game to some extent and be willing to play. That willingness can be negatively influenced if the relationship is not good (enough) or if there are negative emotions before or during the negotiation process. For example, in situations in which not profit but loss must be shared or where there is so little room for negotiation that one or both of the parties will end up below their point of resistance, a conflict is waiting to happen. There is no more motion in the negotiation and the positions become fixed or move apart rather than closer together. If you notice that you are winding up in the conflict spiral, it is important to move in the direction of a value adding negotiation: stop defending your position and look for your mutual interests. In general, that has a de-escalating effect. It is also possible that you have to shift back to the emotion or hidden opposition and influence level before you can return to a constructive conversation.

Examples

A medium-sized law firm is considering having its vehicle fleet managed by a leasing company via a sale-and-lease-back-construction as opposed to managing it themselves. Subjects of discussion (the issues) include the discount percentage on the lease rates, the number of cars that are included in the deal and the trade-in price for the existing vehicle fleet.

Opening

In response to the other party's opening move:
Buyer: 'Good. Let's talk about the terms. I have looked at your proposal with regard to the prices you are offering for the cars. I have to say your offer is somewhat disappointing.'
Salesperson: 'What did you have in mind?'
Buyer: 'If we assume you are buying-up ten employee cars, then based on the Auto Club trade-in price guide, I come up with a total purchase price of 84,000 euro. That is over 30,000 euro more than your offer. Furthermore, I expect a discount of around ten percent on your standard lease rates.'
Salesperson: 'The rates which we offered do not conform to our standard terms: in the contract as we see it, they have already been adjusted. The money has to come from somewhere. The offer seems fair to me.'

Signals from both negotiators:
Buyer: 'If you will not meet me in any other way, then I am afraid we will not come to an agreement. Based on the offer as it now stands, it is impossible for me to accept.'
Salesperson: 'Naturally, I cannot meet you on all fronts. What is the

most important to you? As long as we are not managing your entire vehicle fleet, I cannot go any lower on the lease rates.'

Concessions without asking for anything in return

Example A:
Salesperson: 'Okay, I think I can go along with your reasoning. What would you say if I add 10,000 euro to the buy-up price? Then you have to admit that you are getting quite a sum for your existing fleet!'
Buyer: 'That is quite a big step. Thanks! If you add another 5,000 euro then I think I can convince my boss that we have to be happy with a five percent discount on the lease rates rather than ten percent.'

In this example the salesperson is giving away 10,000 euro without asking for anything in return. The effect of this is that the buyer smells her chance. She plays the 'thank-and-bank-card' and grabs the concession without giving anything back. Immediately on top of that she makes a conditional concession, in which she keeps her options open by passing the buck to her boss. The salesperson has therefore got nowhere with her concession of 10,000 euro.

Example B:
Buyer: 'In principle I wouldn't mind talking about the entire vehicle fleet.'
Salesperson: 'Great! It is easier for us both to talk about the complete package.'
Buyer: 'What about the ten percent discount?'
Salesperson: 'I can't go there. As I said: you are already getting a good rate. If you want to agree with my buy-up total, then I can take off another two percent.'

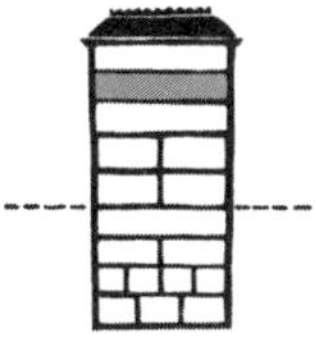

In this example, the buyer does not realize how big a concession the entire vehicle fleet is for the salesperson. The salesperson is smart enough not to let on how happy he is with this by passing it off as a practical point. The concession has then in fact been made and accepted. With that, the buyer loses an important bargaining chip with which she could have got a bigger discount. The salesperson however proposes a conditional concession.

Conditional concessions

Example A:
Salesperson: 'If you were prepared to accept the lease rate, then I might be able to do something about the buy-up sum.'
Buyer: 'What could you do?'
Salesperson: 'Will you agree to the lease rate?'
Buyer: 'No. If I lower my demand from a ten percent to five percent discount what would that mean for the buy-up sum?'
Salesperson: 'Then I could raise the buy-up sum by 10,000 euro.'

Here the salesperson starts off with a careful signal rather than a concrete concession. Despite the fact that the buyer baits him with a clever question, the salesperson continues playing the conditional game. The possible concession will only be given at the moment when the discount on the lease rate is decreased.

Example B:
Buyer: 'I would be willing to set the entire fleet on the table if I get a decent discount for it.'
Salesperson: 'What do you think is decent?'
Buyer: 'The ten percent I mentioned earlier.'
Salesperson: 'Okay, so a ten percent discount on the lease rate and

we get your entire vehicle fleet?'
Buyer: 'Good, let's look at the buy-up sum again.'

Here too we see a signal first. The requested concession is clearly articulated, and both parties agree to the trade: ten percent discount for transferring the entire vehicle fleet to the leasing company.

End game

Example without conditional end concessions and a check on the mandate:
Salesperson: 'Okay, as far as I can tell, we are pretty much in agreement. The last thing I can do is offer 5,000 euro more for the vehicle fleet, but that's it.'
Buyer: 'So your proposal is the deal as we have discussed it and an extra 5,000 euro for the buy-up sum?'
Salesperson: 'Yes, can we close the deal?'
Buyer: 'No, I have to think about it!'

Example with conditional end concession and a check on the mandate:
Salesperson: 'Okay, as far as I can tell, we are pretty much in agreement. I am still talking to the person who makes the final decision, right?'
Buyer: 'Certainly.'
Salesperson: 'So if we reach an agreement, then we can sign the deal today?'
Buyer: 'Yes we can.'
Salesperson: 'Can we wrap up the deal right now?'
Buyer: 'With an extra 5,000 euro on the buy-up sum you have a deal.'

Salesperson: 'If you sign now, then I can give you another 2,000 euro, but you are raking me over the coals!'
Buyer: '2,500 euro?'
Salesperson: 'Deal!'

Issue management

Issue management - creating alternatives:
Salesperson: 'As long as it isn't clear what part of the vehicle fleet you want to replace, it is difficult to offer you the best terms.'
Buyer: 'Let's say for now all fifteen.'
Salesperson: 'Okay, say we go for all fifteen cars: we maximize the buy up sum at 90,000 euro which you can pocket immediately and we raise the lease rate five percent above what is stated in the proposal. How does that sound?'
Buyer: 'Increase it above the proposed rate; I don't think so!'
Salesperson: 'And if we do things completely differently: if you receive the buy up sum all at once, it means a big tax disadvantage. After all, the total will be immediately calculated as part of your profits this year.'
Buyer: 'Only the portion above the book value.'
Salesperson: 'That's 50,000 euro. If, for example, you were prepared to entirely give up the buy up sum, then I can extend a discount of 35 percent on the lease rates for the first two years.'
Buyer: '35 percent? Well, I'll have to think about that!'

In this example you see that the salesperson has already converted his issues to euros. This puts him in a position to play with various issues and trade these off against one another. And he is thinking along with his client and showing her the different possibilities. This gives him more insight into the client's world and the degree to which she values the various options.

Issue management – reducing complexity:

- 'We are talking about rates for all the cars separately. Maybe it would be better if we work with one discount percentage for the entire vehicle fleet?'
- 'Let's look at deals for the coming year. We can always come back and make agreements for next year at a later date.'

Issue management – increasing solution room:

- 'Let's look at the fiscal side of the options.'
- 'Maybe we should first decide if we can reach an acceptable agreement about the cars for staff members. We can talk about cars for the partners and the director after that.'
- 'Let's look at the total cost for the entire term rather than only for the first year.'

Reducing conflict – from positions to interests:

Buyer: 'I want an extra ten percent discount or you can just forget it!'
Salesperson: 'I cannot offer you that, I will not go over five percent.'
Buyer: 'Good, then I will go back to talking with your competitor.'
Salesperson: 'Let's stop talking about percentages for a minute: what is this really about?'
Buyer: 'Ultimately I want good service and a reliable partner; I just don't want to pay too much for it!'
Salesperson: 'I can imagine that. We would like to build up a long term relationship with you which benefits us both. Of course, I do have to make a healthy margin on the deal. That's what keeps us in business after all.'
Buyer: 'Well, then we should be able to work something out. Maybe we have to look at an open calculation?'
Salesperson: 'That would definitely be a possibility.'

Negotiation tricks

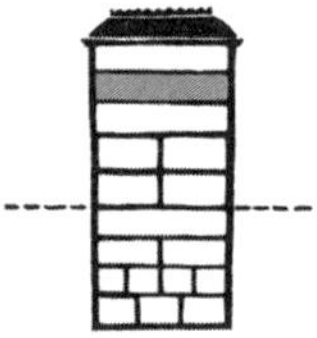

In value sharing negotiations you run the risk that your negotiation partner will try to play tricks on you. It is essential for you to have this insight because once you have seen through a trick, it loses its effect. The most important types of tricks are:

1. Influencing perception
2. Withholding information
3. Working with emotion
4. Working with time
5. Team tricks

Influencing perception

Maximizing/minimizing

With this trick, the other person blows up the value of their concessions while belittling concessions you make.

Example:
'So I am doing my best here to ensure that you supply us not only with paperclips, but also plastic cups, pens, tape and printer paper – which more than doubles your turnover with us – and the best you can do is come up with a measly two percent extra discount?'

Dealing with this trick

Your most important weapon against this trick is recognition. If you see the other person using this trick, you can consider doing the same. You can identify the behaviour or just ignore it; you can also calmly refer back to the purpose of the conversation.

Emphasize dependence on the other person

With this trick, the negotiator attempts to increase your willingness to make concessions by creating the impression that they would not mind if you do not reach an agreement. In actuality, this is a misuse of a BATNA. This trick is often employed by bluffers without a true underlying BATNA.

Example:

'Listen here. I am going to spend ten more minutes trying to make an acceptable deal with you and after that I am going to spend my time with one of your competitors.'

Dealing with this trick

Your most important weapon against this trick is the realization that you, just like your negotiation partner, are free to choose not to make a deal. It can be clarifying and refreshing if you react calmly when being confronted by this trick. Setting limits, identifying the manipulation or simply emphasizing that both parties need an acceptable solution are also effective tactics to handle this trick.

'That is just how it works'

This trick – 'that is just how it works in our organization' – is often used by negotiators in large companies or institutions. They often have rules or procedures which they, according to what they say, cannot deviate from, even for you. Thus the rules of the game are dictated by factors which apparently cannot be changed and which enable the other party to achieve the upper hand. A variant of this trick is often used with overbooked flights or hotels ('you will be staying in a hotel just up the road, sir). You are continually asked for one sided concessions due to the rules or circumstances.

Example:

- 'We never give discounts.'
- 'A sixty day payment term is a requirement for all permanent contracts.'

Dealing with this trick

Just as with the previous trick, you yourself determine which proposal you wish to commit to. Remember that in general, everything is negotiable so you never have to just go along with an 'absolute fact.' Naturally, you can consider assenting to the standard rules of your negotiation partner, but my advice is to treat this like all the other issues in the negotiation. If for example your negotiation partner insists on a long payment term, it might mean fewer discounts. That is when issue management is appropriate. The now familiar motto 'give nothing away without obtaining something in return' is true here as well. When presented with a tough line like 'we never give discounts,' it is nice to set your own limits, for example: 'I never buy anything without a discount.' Another possibility is simply not to agree to what your negotiation partner demands and to leave the responsibility for the demand up to them.

Withholding information

Misinformation

Negotiators can play with information in any number of ways. They even think of strategies to present the other person with supposed misunderstandings. 'Leaking' incorrect information is a trick to be wary of.

Dealing with this trick

Never buy into relevant professional information if it comes from possibly corrupted sources. Be cautious at all times and continually test all assumptions. See also the section about preparation: know what you don't know in negotiation.

Informing tactically

The negotiator who is prepared, or is obliged to divulge all the information, and, for instance, may need a fiat from elsewhere, is still able to make a tactical choice about the moment when they divulge the whole story.

Example:
John: 'Hi Erica, one of your clients asked me to give a half day presentation during a company outing. Any problems with that?'
Erica: 'Um no, of course not.'
John: 'Okay thanks, then I'll go ahead with it. By the way, it's in Bali!'

Dealing with this trick

After your negotiation partner has added the extra information, a new situation arises in point of fact. That means that there is absolutely no reason why you have to uphold your previous decision. My advice is if something similar happens to you, reverse your authorization. This also applies if costs have been incurred or if you have to come back on previously made agreements. A person who uses this trick is well aware of their actions and should be held responsible for all the problems arising from this way of informing others.

You can arm yourself against this trick by asking multiple questions before agreeing to a proposal. Every approval you give represents value. Be as careful with this as with spending money!

Misunderstanding

With this trick, a misunderstanding is used underhandedly: your negotiation partner acts as though they are under the impression that a specific concession has been made and sometimes negotiates accordingly. When later it turns out that you have not made the concession at all, they play the victim and pretend that there has been a misunderstanding and they understood things differently.

Example:
Upon discovering a misunderstanding:
'Hey, wait a minute. You were going to cover the logistics costs, right? I will never be able to sell this story. Even worse, I was never authorized to make the deal like this. I thought we had settled everything already?!'

Dealing with this trick
The success of this trick lies in people's tendency to lose focus when they feel they have reached a good agreement on the wrapping up and closing deals level. They are so relieved about the results accomplished that they want to finish up as quickly as possible in order to enjoy their success. For this reason, many agreements are not confirmed in writing which means that, later on, there is no evidence. If you tend to be swept along in your relief, there is a chance that you will make concessions which you will later regret. Don't do it! You can consider insisting on the original agreement. If you do not, then the negotiation must in fact begin all over. Make sure you get your fair piece of the pie!

Blitzkrieg
This trick is used at the beginning of a tense negotiation. When you least expect it, in an almost friendly manner, a tricky negotiator plays an issue out of your hands which you might have used to your advantage later in the negotiation but which you didn't want to be difficult about in the beginning. In this way they grab a concession before the negotiation has even got off the ground.

Example:
'Hello Linda, sit down. We are going to talk about the conditions of your upcoming departure from our organization. But first I wanted to say this: it does not seem like you have a lot to do between now and

your departure date, so you could easily use your vacation time. What we still have to discuss is...'

In this case the vacation time could have been an important issue in the further negotiations.

Dealing with this trick
My advice is to always view agreements as provisional until a complete outline is made. Do not make any partial agreements. If you indicate that you will give definite permission only on a complete agreement, then in a similar situation you do not have to worry about a subtopic.

Higher power
A nasty but effective trick is referring to a 'higher power' at the end of a negotiation. In this way, the negotiation result is brought back to the first qualifying round. Worse yet: if the higher power comes back with a negative response, the other party is pressured to come up with a more favourable proposition.

Example:
'Well, that seems to be good deal. I will pitch it to my boss.'

Dealing with this trick
You can arm yourself against this trick by checking if your negotiation partner has a sufficient mandate to reach a deal with you at the very start of the negotiation. If that is not the case, then there is little use in negotiating with them. Parallel to that, it is not wise to begin a negotiation if an important person, for whatever reason, is not yet present. If, despite your alertness, you are confronted with this trick at the end of a negotiation, then you can respond to that by asking

the other person what they personally think of the agreement reached. Subsequently, you can indicate that you are not pleased with the way things are going and that a complex situation will arise if the agreement must be approved by someone higher up. The rule applies here as well: do not make any concessions without getting something in return! The best response to this trick is to refuse to continue talking with your negotiation partner until the boss comes to the table, when you will in fact have to begin a new negotiation. The advantage of this is that this new round offers new opportunities: in addition to new demands, new concessions are in all likelihood possible, which ultimately may lead to a better deal for you both.

Working with emotion

Emotional manipulation is a commonly used negotiation trick. You can find examples of positive and negative emotional manipulation in chapter 14.

Working with time

Now or never

Sometimes a negotiator increases the pressure by linking an offer or a concession to a time limit. This trick is often used by salespeople. The effect of this trick is greatest if the time limit is not set by the salesperson, but 'imposed by circumstances.'

Example:
'I can offer this refrigerator to you today for 1,500 euro. Tomorrow, new prices go into effect and I cannot deviate from them. Personally, I think it's a little ridiculous, but in any case, you can still take advantage of the low prices today.'

Dealing with this trick

This trick indicates that your negotiation partner wants to make a deal with you. There is a big chance that you can actually improve on the terms of the agreement because they probably have some extra wiggle room. It is also possible of course that something is not right here. You must always be on your guard when someone uses this trick!

The most important thing is that you do not allow yourself to be flustered by this trick. Take the time for discussion and decision making, despite the ultimatum. If after the designated deadline you ask for the same (or even better) terms, in most cases you will get them.

Delay

With this trick, negotiations are drawn out as long as possible so that the other person feels pressured by time and, in an attempt to conclude things, makes concessions.

Example:

Buyer: 'I am in a hurry because I have a board meeting shortly. We still have to talk about your rates because I feel they are still a little high.'

Salesperson: 'Okay, then I will explain to you what's included in the rate so you have a better idea of the value you are getting.' (subsequently spends nearly ten minutes on the explanation while the buyer gets more and more impatient.)

Buyer: 'I really have to go now. I'll just approve these rates, but I don't want to see any extra costs this year or next year either. I'm being really nice by doing this!'

Salesperson: 'Agreed. Thanks.'

Dealing with this trick

If you are going to conduct an important negotiation, then schedule it so that it can run overtime. That way you remove possible time pressure for yourself. If you still do not have enough time,

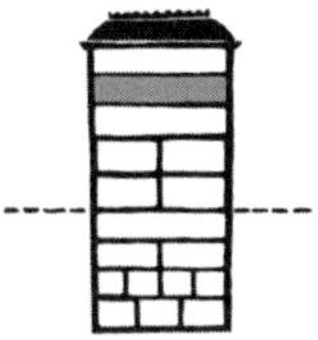

then it helps not to state your absolute deadline for finishing. That eliminates the possibility that the other person might abuse your timeframe. Should you catch the other person consciously delaying the negotiation, then you can let them know you know that. If you can permit it and you really mean it, you can even go so far as to give the other person an ultimatum. In any case, do not reward time pressure with concessions from your side!

Oops, forgot!

If once negotiations are completed the negotiator introduces extra points, it is usually a way to pressure you. You want to uphold the deal and because of this you will be inclined to make extra concessions.

Example:
'Good, we've worked it out. Oh yeah, the curtains and such are part of the deal, right?'

Dealing with this trick

The same tips described earlier in the 'misunderstanding trick' apply here as well. Always wrap up your negotiation solidly, confirm agreements in writing and do not make one sided concessions, before or afterwards.

Team tricks

Good guy, bad guy

The oldest trick in the book is still used successfully. One team member is unyielding and often quite emotional. The other one is kind enough to calm her teammate down and seems friendlier than she actually is: she worms significant concessions out of you under cover of 'helping' so that she can finish her 'good' work.

Example:
Player 1: 'I wouldn't want to rent you this office if you were the last client on earth. The price is 400 euro per square meter and if you can't afford that, it's just too bad.'
Player 2: 'Peter, calm down! Sorry sir, maybe it's better if we continue this conversation alone. I believe that your opening offer fell on deaf ears. I will see what I can do for you. You would help me out by upping your offer just a little, if, that is, your budget allows. I think that that will help me smooth out the negotiation process. What do you think of that?'

Dealing with this trick
This trick no longer works as soon as you indicate that you have seen through your negotiation partners' game.

Breaking up assigned roles
This trick is aimed at breaking up the prearranged roles within your team in order to irritate you and create confusion. Most negotiation teams have pre-assigned roles: one is spokesperson for a specific subject and the other one for a different subject. Additionally, one of the team members is usually in charge. The trick is fairly simple: the other team breaks up the assigned roles by posing questions to the wrong person, interrupting the person speaking and focusing attention on the least experienced and least important member of the team.

Dealing with this trick
First of all, before you sit down with your negotiation partner(s), agreements have to be made within your team concerning the content and course of the negotiation. Next, during the negotiation, never let the other team drive your team apart. Do not be afraid to take a time-out to discuss the state of affairs within your team. Repeat role assignments and decisions about who talks about what as

often as necessary. In team negotiations it also works well to let one person do all the talking.

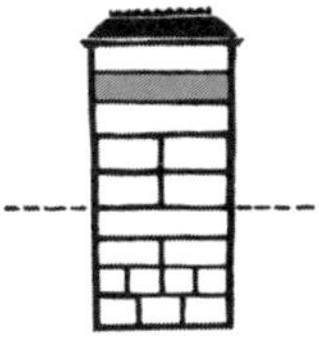

Divide and conquer

The last trick goes a bit further than the previous one and is aimed at playing members of the same team against each other. Since most members of negotiation teams have individual interests in addition to team interests, addressing the individual interests of one or more of the team members will almost certainly cause stress for the other team member(s).

Dealing with this trick

Make sure that all the individual interests of you and your team members are considered in an agreed-upon team position. That might mean that the negotiations within your team can last longer and be more difficult than the ultimate negotiation between the teams. During internal negotiations, ensure that solutions are found which equally serve the interests of all the team members. Tips to defend yourself against 'breaking up assigned roles' also apply here.

Advantages and risks

The whole process of value sharing negotiations shows that personal interest is the primary basic principle. Concern for the other person is usually absent, as is the intention to create a fair deal for all those involved. It is a tough, sometimes brutal manner to reach a solution, which means negotiations, especially concerning complex issues, can easily turn into conflicts. If it is not possible to come closer together, a battle of positions threatens to arise in which the negotiation partners, without listening to one another, toss opinions at each another and dig themselves deeper into a hole. Furthermore, value sharing negotiations leave little room for creativity because there is often an atmosphere of 'every word counts.' This can stop people from communicating freely, with the consequence that creative processes are obstructed. Exploration and adding value do not therefore have any explicit place in value sharing negotiations. This is a pity because value can be lost in this way.

Value sharing negotiations are extra risky in long term relationships in which a conflict is undesirable, in situations where there is lots of room for exploration, but also when they involve complex issues. My advice is: try – if really important and complicated interests are at stake – to reach an agreement by using value adding negotiation techniques. On the other hand, a value sharing negotiation can lead to a mutually acceptable agreement quickly and without too many complications for people who are familiar with the game. Value sharing negotiations are mainly suited to negotiations in which the sharing aspect is more important than adding value. In relatively simple (commercial) situations it can be the best manner to negotiate. Because the risk of being deceived – characteristic of value sharing negotiations – is slight, this manner of negotiation is mainly interesting with large negotiation values. The original position is only abandoned after mature consideration and in exchange for well thought out concessions. With onetime contact, the value sharing method is often implemented because the consequences of a possible conflict in the long term are much less serious.

Next steps

If you have brought your negotiation to an agreement, you can continue on to the level of wrapping up and closing deals in order to lay out all the agreements made and conclude the negotiation (chapter 31). If you were unable to come to an agreement, you can still choose to conclude the conversation. Certainly if you do not see any room for further negotiation, it is better to end the conversation than to continue on too long and irritate your conversation partner. If you have the idea that an agreement is still possible, you can go back to the value adding negotiations/problem solving level to examine further options.

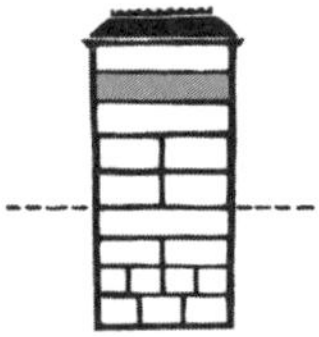

Difficulty with value sharing negotiations?

Do you have trouble (continuing) with tough value sharing negotiations? Then you may recognize yourself in one of the following stereotypes.

"I can't negotiate"
Many people have trouble with the 'knife-on-the-table-atmosphere' which is often present in value sharing negotiations. A common reaction is that they avoid the confrontation by pulling back or just allowing someone else to take over the negotiation. Possibly the biggest problem in (all) negotiations is the fact that people convince themselves that they just can't do it. That is too easy! It is true that negotiations are tricky and not without risks, but you can always say 'no' or ask for time to think about what you have been offered. And if you are just not happy with the proposition and you don't see any room for improvement, then you can of course turn the proposal down.

Finally: if you feel that you are a bad negotiator, then it is essential that you do not try and please the other person immediately and on all points. Try and find the strength to chart your own course!

Difficult to survey
As you saw in the examples, it can be rather complicated to conduct a good sharing oriented negotiation. You need knowledge of the issues, good preparation – and preferably a big helping of experience as well. But do you know any way to get that experience without getting your fingers burned once in a while?

Sticking up for yourself
An important condition of value sharing negotiations is that you have

to be able to stand up for your personal interests unashamedly. Many people have to get used to that idea. Lots of us learn early on that it is not proper to openly stand up for our own interests. And yet, negotiating is something we do from a young age. You can bet that when it came to bedtime, sweets and toys, we used to be very clear about our personal interests and knew how to serve them just fine. Even now we usually know pretty much what we want and what we need from other people, even if it is not always easy to determine right away, let alone get. Value sharing negotiations are a fairly open and sincere manner to get what we need and therefore should have preference above all sorts of hidden manipulative tricks. But you have to have everything ordered, be able to make choices and be prepared to live with the consequences.

31

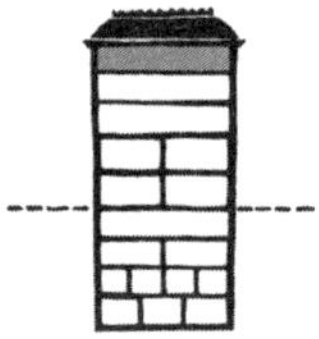

Level +4: wrapping up and closing deals

If you have conducted a conversation on one or more of the conversation levels between -4 and +3, then you – if all went well – have achieved results. In order to be sure that the results as you see them match up with the results perceived by your conversation partner, you once again summarize the outcome at the end of the conversation and check that your agreements are indeed mutually accepted. That clarifies what you can expect of each other in the future. Next you record your agreement, preferably in writing, to prevent any confusion about the deal from arising in the future. If necessary, you can make supplementary deals regarding a follow up to your conversation.

A good conclusion is vitally important because if you do not explicitly conclude a conversation, there is a chance that much of the potential result may be lost.

Practical tips

In wrapping up a conversation it is a good idea to reflect on the goals (concrete, relationship oriented and process related) which you originally had in mind and address them. For concrete goals, summarize agreements made as completely as possible. As far as the relationship goes, a more general note will suffice; the atmosphere with which you are concluding business often says enough about the condition of the relationship. Referring to the process, indicate where you are now and try to reach an agreement about the next step.

Examples

Substantive:

A: 'Okay. This is what I understand: we will foot the bill for transportation. The travel insurance will be taken care of by your organization. The pieces will remain with our exhibition for two months and we will look after insurance during this period. As compensation, you will receive 10,000 euro in advance. Have I left anything out?'

B: 'Yes, from when to when does the exhibition run exactly?'

A: 'From 6 May through 30 June.'

B: 'Okay, then the pieces will be returned in early July?'

A: 'Indeed. Shall I record the agreements on paper?'

Relationship:

A: 'I am so pleased that we were able to look each other in the eye and discuss our long-standing difficulties so openly. What did you think?'

B: 'I have a lot of respect for openness, but we need to eliminate our problems once and for all and that hasn't happened yet.'

A: 'Shall we plan a meeting to talk about that in the near future?'

Process:

A: 'Okay, you've had the chance to closely examine our situation. Do you have any questions?'

B: 'No, I think I have a lot of information. May I contact you if I come up with something?'

A: 'Of course. When do you think you will have the offer ready?'

B: 'In two weeks, is that quick enough for you?'

A: 'Fine. Let's make an appointment right now for two weeks hence.'

Difficulty with wrapping up?

The only real problem which might come up during the wrapping up phase has to do with acting too hastily. There are different reasons to be in a hurry at the end of a discussion. It may be that your conversation went overtime which means you do not have a lot of time. It might also be that you are impatient or are quick to be satisfied with an insufficiently crystallized result. Insecurity can also be a cause of wrapping up too quickly. Once you have reached an agreement, you may be so relieved that you end the conversation before it is actually concluded. Your insecurity can also be expressed by fear of the fact that the other person will go back on their word – and you don't want to give them time to do so. Try to resist these pitfalls and take the time to line up all the agreements you have made.

Acknowledgements

In writing this book I have thought a lot about three special people whom I would like to thank for their vision and inspiration:

Cees Lips, former head master of the Utrechts Stedelijk Gymnasium, who showed me the difference between a debate and a dialogue and also the power of reason and the great importance of personal integrity. His influence can mainly be found in the basic principles.

Ton de Leeuw, professor emeritus in business administration at the Rijksuniversiteit in Groningen. He taught me to apply system analysis to complex and dynamic systems as well as the importance of model formation and empirical testing. His influence can be noted in the structured aspect of the model and the fact that every instruction which you find in this book has been extensively tested in practice.

Johan Kos, Pathwork helper and coach, who taught me that the (difficult) situations we find ourselves in are to a large extent of our own creation; that interactions with others, especially when they get hard, offer excellent opportunities for personal insights and that the acceptance of imperfection, in ourselves and in others, is an important key to growth. His influence can especially be seen in parts which discuss personal development based on the winning dialogue system.

Furthermore, many thanks to Joop Rijsterborgh of Philips Consumer Electronics, who – on behalf of his account managers – first asked the questions which lead to the development of the winning dialogue system.

I would also like to mention Arie van der Giessen and Titia Roovers – who contributed to the development of the book in the early stages – and Johan van der Tas, David de Vriend, Michiel Castelijns,

Stéphanie Grimmelt, Willy Zelen, Cees van Halem, Marieke Textor and Mark de Vos – all of whom critically read through the manuscript at different times – I am grateful for their input. And thank you, Stephenie Harris-Adama, Nicole Westerwoudt and Desirée van der Kuijl; you did a great job of translating the manuscript into English.

In addition to those directly involved, many colleagues and clients of InContext Consultancy Group, each in their own way, contributed to the development and honing of the system and associated tips and suggestions.

Finally, I would like to particularly thank Birgitte Broersma and Hetty Jongenelen for months of patient editing, great care for the ideas and principles of the winning dialogue and the ultimate realization of a readable and comprehensive whole.

Thomas Benedict

Bibliography

Covey, S.R. (2000). *The seven habits of highly effective people.* Amsterdam: Business Contact. Twaalfde druk.

Covey, S.R. (2005). *The 8th habit.* From effectiveness to greatness. Amsterdam: Business Contact.

Engel, J.F., R.D. Blackwell & P.W. Miniard (1986). *Consumer behaviour.* Londen: The Dryden Press. Vijfde druk.

Fisher, R. & W. Ury (1994). *Getting to yes; the secret to successful negotiation.* Amsterdam: Business Contact. Vijftiende druk.

Leeuw, A.C.J. de (1986). *Organisaties: management, analyse, ontwerp en verandering; een systeemvisie.* Assen: Van Gorcum.

Maister, D.H. (1997). *True Professionalism.* New York: The Free Press.

Mastenbroek, W.F.G. (1996). *Conflicthantering en organisatieontwikkeling.* Alphen aan den Rijn/Deurne: Samsom. Tweede druk.

Mastenbroek, W.F.G. (2004a). *Onderhandelen.* Utrecht: Het Spectrum. Vijftiende druk.

Mastenbroek, W.F.G. (2004b). *Vaardiger onderhandelen.* Heemstede: Holland Business Publications. Zesde druk.

Nalebuff, A. & B. Brandenburger (1996). *Spelen met de concurrent.* Amsterdam: Business Contact.

Pruitt, D. & P.J. Carnevale (1993). *Negotiation in social conflict.* Buckingham, Engeland: Open University Press.

Ryan, K.D. & D.K. Oestreich (1991). *Driving fear out of the workplace: creating the high-trust, high-performance organization.* San Francisco: Jossey-Bass.

Skinner, B.F. (1966). *The behavior of organisms.* New York: Appleton-Century-Crofts.

Tolle, E. (2005). *De kracht van het nu.* Deventer: Ankh-Hermes. Elfde druk.

Vrolijk, A. (1997). *Gesprekstechniek.* Houten/Diegem: Bohn Stafleu Van Loghum. Eerste druk, zesde oplage.

Appendix 1

Table 1 gives you an idea of the complete winning dialogue system, with a summary of relevant factors for each level. You can use this overview to prepare for your conversations, to anticipate unexpected events, to choose your approach and to develop possible alternative scenarios.

	Starting point	Goal	Posture suggestion
+4 Wrapping up and closing deals	When you have a content related agreement, you can take the step to decision making. If you have discussed all the agenda points, you can conclude the conversation.	• Clarifying what you have achieved for both parties and making agreements definite.	• Remain focused on the person and the relationship.
+3 Value sharing negotiations	After investigating the possibility of merging interests, opposing interests may remain.	• Finding a mutually acceptable solution to negotiation points which do not lend themselves to resolution via value adding methods.	• Look for an honest division of tasks and rewards so that a win-win situation is still possible. • Always be aware of the option not to close the deal.
+2 Value adding negotiations	There are problems or divergent interests and a solution is needed. It is not yet clear how much interests overlap one another.	• Looking for mutually beneficial solutions in which both parties achieve their highest goals without making concessions. • Exploring room to solve problems without making concessions.	• Be open to creative solutions. • Keep looking for mutually beneficial possibilities. • Where possible, choose a long term perspective.
+1 Exchanging information	**Persuasion and advice** When you have a good view of the situation and the other person's needs and they acknowledge this fact, you can recommend suggestions/solutions.	• Acquiring acceptance for your ideas/suggestions.	• Show enthusiasm. • Be patient and helpful.
	Providing information If you have information the other person does not, you can give them the relevant facts.	• Helping the other person to receive and understand your information.	• Focus on the information needs and interests of the other person.
	Listening/receiving information In order to exchange valuable information during a conversation it is important to find out what the other person knows and thinks.	• Gathering information. • Understanding the other person. • Building trust and a relationship. • Building credibility.	• Concentrate on what the other person is saying. • Put yourself in their place.
0 Introducing structure	**Conversation opening or intermediate procedure proposal** Each conversation begins with introducing structure. Additionally, corrective action may be necessary as a result of: • A large number of topics; • Conversation partners who interrupt one another.	• Reaching agreement about conversation topics and the sequence in which they will be discussed.	• Be professional. • Focus on the other person's interests.

Behaviour suggestion	Pitfalls	Solutions
• Summarize the entire conversation and check understanding and acceptance. • If necessary make agreements about subsequent steps.	• Assuming too quickly that you are agreed. • Losing focus.	• Consciously take the time for this phase; be alert to the danger of vague agreements.
• Look for objective criteria for sharing. • Discuss various scenarios. • Open and close negotiation issues. • Calculate the value of different options. • Only accept win-win agreements. • Make conditional concessions based on the low cost, high benefit principle.	• One sided concessions. • Making the negotiation into a fight.	• Never give something away which you get nothing for in return. • Guard content related and behavioural limits.
• Separate conceptualizing and deciding, and postpone definitive decisions. • Look for interests rather than positions. • Generate mutually beneficial alternatives.	• Holding on to a standpoint/ solution rather than focusing on interests.	• Focus on actual interests. • Think about alternatives; keep options open.
• Link suggestions to established needs and preferences. • Articulate the advantages of your ideas/ suggestions for the other person.	• Persuading too quickly/too enthusiastically. • Reasoning too much from your own perspective. • Getting into an argument regarding objections/ resistance.	• Maintain contact. • Remain helpful and do not let your own interests get the upper hand. • Shift back to level -2.
• Link to existing knowledge. • Structure your information. • Give vibrant examples.	• Giving too much information. • Explaining to make an impression/ convince yourself. • The other person quits. • The other person works against you.	• Match your behaviour to the goal. • Restore the connection. • Find out what is going on; shift back to level -3.
• Listen actively: encourage, ask questions, and summarize content and feelings. • Begin with a general, open-ended question and work towards specific points. • Let the other person finish speaking before you continue.	• Getting into an argument/giving your own opinion. • You receive short answers/ the conversation falls silent. • The other person gets irritated.	• Stay with the other person. • Work on your questioning technique. • Summarize (feelings). • Continue questioning rather than asking new questions. • Have you earned the right to broach the subject? • Does the other person know that/ why it is in his best interest to answer the questions?
• Summarize when necessary. • Make your suggestion and point out the advantages to the other person. • Make sure your conversation partner agrees with the proposed structure.	• Reacting too fast to the content. • The other person responds to the content immediately. • The other person has other ideas about the structure.	• Prepare yourself well. • Keep an eye on the procedure. • Carefully request thought to the structure. • Merge the two suggestions into a new structure.

	Other person's behaviour provocation	Negative needs win-lose/lose-lose	Positive needs win-win
-1 Resistance	• Little reaction. • Shaking of the head, leaning back, arms crossed. • 'Yes, but…'	• Closed to influence.	• Involved with the proposal. • Attempt to get clearer information. • Look for a connection between personal interests and proposal made.
-2 Emotion	**Emotion** • Screaming, crying, silence. • Exaggerated demands and accusations.	• Fostering sympathy. • Sabotaging conversation progress.	• Expressing emotion.
	Criticism and complaints • Negative remarks about you, your behaviour, your product, your colleague or the organization you work for.	• Getting revenge. • Belittling you. • Negotiation position.	• Expressing dissatisfaction. • Bring up mistakes. • Giving feedback. • Starting the improvement process.
-3 Hidden opposition and manipulation	**Lack of commitment** • Passiveness. • Indifference. • No participation in the conversation. • Irritating remarks. • You can't get a foot in the door.	• Sabotaging. • Avoiding confrontation. • Getting revenge.	• Getting acknowledgement. • Only start a conversation if there is a good basis for one. • Justification for your own feelings of anger, irritation or distrust.
	Negative behaviour • Not cooperating in the conversation. • Irritating remarks. • Quitting.	• Sabotaging.	• Discussing state of affairs. • Expressing powerlessness. • Getting lack of commitment on the table.
	Manipulation • Flattery, which belittles the other person. • Show of power to increase your insecurity. • Creative variants are possible.	• Figurative influence on your decisions.	• Obtain influence over the situation.
-4 Aggression	**Aggression due to powerlessness** • Cursing. • Personal attack. • Conditional threats.	• Getting revenge. • Belittling you.	• Obtain influence over the situation.
	Intimidation Indirect threats.	• Using fear to make you more accommodating.	N/a
	Physical violence or direct threats Short, fierce orders.	• Exercising power. • Forcing preferences.	N/a

Posture suggestion	Behaviour suggestion	Watch out for
• Involvement and interest in the other person. • If you want to be heard, you must be willing to listen.	• Sense. • Encourage. • Clarify. • Acknowledge • Respond.	• Persuading too quickly. • Saying 'Yes, but…' yourself. • Allowing feelings of frustration, tension and impatience to get the upper hand. • Shouting down resistance. • Ignoring resistance.
• Make space for the other person.	• Listen. • Summarize feelings. • Show understanding. • Wait until pressure is gone to ask questions.	• Getting down to business too quickly. • Making a content related response to emotional standpoints. • See also: criticism and complaints.
• Take in everything and reserve judgement for later. • Accept your own responsibility.	• Listen and confirm. • Show that you take the remarks seriously. • Is an apology warranted?	• Agreeing just to get it over with. • Passing blame. • Defending. • Justifying. • Hitting back: 'Yes, but you…'
• Try to understand your conversation partner. • View your own role critically. • Allow yourself to be vulnerable. • Try to relieve tension.	• Acknowledge the other person's feelings. • Try to get the other person to talk about what is bothering him. • Apologize when necessary or express sympathy. • Make your (good) intentions clear.	• Impatience or anger. • Making accusations. • Avoiding 'old injuries.'
• Be firm.	• Stop the conversation. • Identify behaviour and its consequences. • Ask for an explanation. • Make agreements.	• Allowing irritation to escalate without discussing it. • Continuing without commitment from the other person.
• Stay in touch with your feelings. • Never make concessions under (emotional) pressure.	• Do not buy into manipulation. • Refer to the actual topics of conversation. • Interrupt if necessary. • See also: negative behaviour.	• Feelings of superiority, inferiority or dependence which stand in the way of clear thinking.
• Calm yet clear.	• Indicate what possibilities are (and are not). • Calmly set limits. • Cut off conversation if necessary.	• Authoritarian behaviour. • Disrespectful performance. • Hiding behind rules. • An aggressive response.
• Do not allow yourself to be influenced by fear. • Keep your head cool.	• Do not buy into the intimidation. • Refer to the business at hand.	• Showing fear.
• Restrain yourself.	• Try to relieve tension. • Make yourself small. • Attempt to end the situation.	• Causing violence. • An aggressive response. • Panic. • Heroics.

Table 1 All the stories, characteristics, pitfalls and solutions

Register

About the author

Thomas Benedict studied business administration at the Rijksuniversiteit in Groningen and later completed post doctoral training in management consultancy at the Vrije Universiteit in Amsterdam. For the past fifteen years he has carried out projects worldwide as a trainer and organization advisor in various branches, including fast moving consumer goods, the medical sector, telecommunications and electronics. He is the cofounder and director of InContext Consultancy Group, an organization with around 30 people based in Baarn which assists organizations with vision, strategy, change issues, as well as assessment and competency development. Clients include KPN, Randstad, Achmea, Philips, ING Group, Holland Casino and the Tax Authority. Thomas Benedict regularly publishes articles in daily papers as well as trade journals about the human factor in organizations. Thomas has two children, is passionate about running, sailing and skiing and lives in The Netherlands.

www.incontext.nl
www.thewinningdialogue.com